"So to be able to forgive your ener[emy] [is crucial] to one's spiritual progress?" I asked

"Yes, yes, there is no doubt," he replied. "Its crucial. Its one of the most important things. It can change one's life. To reduce hatred and other destructive emotions, you must develop their opposites—compassion and kindness. If you have strong compassion, strong respect for others, then forgiveness is much easier. Mainly for this reason: I do not want to harm another. Forgiveness allows you to be in touch with these positive emotions. This will help with spiritual development."

"Is there a special meditation technique that you use?" I asked.

"I use a meditation technique called giving and taking," the Dalai Lama explained. "I make visualization: send my positive emotions like happiness, affection to others. Then another visualization. I visualize receiving their sufferings, their negative emotions. I do this every day. I pay special attention to the Chinese—especially those doing terrible things to the Tibetans. So, as I meditate, I breathe in all their poisons—hatred, fear, cruelty. Then I breathe out. And I let all the good things come out, things like compassion, forgiveness. I take inside my body all these bad things. Then I replace poisons with fresh air. Giving and taking. I take care not to blame—I don't blame the Chinese and I don't blame myself. This meditation is very effective, useful to reduce hatred, useful to cultivate forgiveness."

—from *The Wisdom of Forgiveness*

The
WISDOM
of
FORGIVENESS

INTIMATE CONVERSATIONS
AND JOURNEYS

His Holiness the Dalai Lama
and
Victor Chan

Riverhead Books

New York

THE BERKLEY PUBLISHING GROUP
Published by the Penguin Group
Penguin Group (USA) Inc.
375 Hudson Street, New York, New York 10014, USA
Penguin Group (Canada), 10 Alcorn Avenue, Toronto, Ontario M4V 3B2, Canada
(a division of Pearson Penguin Canada Inc.)
Penguin Books Ltd., 80 Strand, London WC2R ORL, England
Penguin Group Ireland, 25 St. Stephen's Green, Dublin 2, Ireland (a division of
Penguin Books Ltd.)
Penguin Group (Australia), 250 Camberwell Road, Camberwell, Victoria 3124, Australia
(a division of Pearson Australia Group Pty. Ltd.)
Penguin Books India Pvt. Ltd., 11 Community Centre, Panchsheel Park, New Delhi—
110 017, India
Penguin Group (NZ), cnr Airborne and Rosedale Roads, Albany, Auckland 1310, New
Zealand (a division of Pearson New Zealand Ltd.)
Penguin Books (South Africa) (Pty.) Ltd., 24 Sturdee Avenue, Rosebank, Johannesburg
2196, South Africa

Penguin Books Ltd., Registered Offices: 80 Strand, London WC2R ORL, England

First Riverhead hardcover edition: August 2004
First Riverhead trade paperback edition: August 2005
Riverhead trade paperback ISBN 1-59448-092-3

The Library of Congress has catalogued the Riverhead hardcover edition as follows:

Bstan-'dzin-rgya-mtsho, Dalai Lama XIV, date.
The wisdom of forgiveness : intimate conversations and journeys / His Holiness the
Dalai Lama and Victor Chan.
p.   cm.
ISBN 1-57322-277-1
1. Bstan-'dzin-rgya-mtsho, Dalai Lama XIV, 1935– —Interviews.   2. Dalai lamas—
Interviews.   3. Bstan-'dzin-rgya-mtsho, Dalai Lama XIV, 1935– —Journeys.
4. Forgiveness—Religious aspects—Buddhism.   5. Compassion—Religious aspects—
Buddhism.   I. Chan, Victor.   II. Title.
BQ7935.B774B77   2004   2004046874
294.3'923'092—dc22

PRINTED IN THE UNITED STATES OF AMERICA

10   9   8   7   6   5   4   3   2   1

Contents

Telepathy in the Prague Castle

I noticed her in the crowd right away. She had pushed herself to the front, just behind the velvet restraining rope in the small banquet hall of the Prague Castle. She was an attractive woman, perhaps in her thirties, with short, blond hair and a purple scarf around her neck. Her face was animated with anticipation.

It was October 2000, and President Václav Havel had invited the Dalai Lama and many of the world's leading thinkers to Prague for a symposium on education and spiritual values. To satisfy numerous requests for interviews, the Tibetan leader had scheduled a press conference. He had just answered a question from a Taiwanese journalist. There were half a dozen of them, and they all wanted to know what the Dalai Lama thought about China and Taiwan.

Then the blond woman took over the portable mike. She leaned forward, two heavy cameras dangling in front of her.

"We are living in the Internet age, and you know so many meditation techniques. I'm sure you're very familiar with telepatee . . ."

"Tela?" The Dalai Lama couldn't understand the word; he looked puzzled.

"Telepatee." She repeated.

"Telepathy." He finally got it.

"Yes . . . Give your thought to another person?" The woman stared intently at the Dalai Lama, her face solemn. From her accent, I guessed that she was either Czech or German.

"Me?" The Dalai Lama roared in his booming baritone, the word resounding in the large, ornate room. The ninety or so journalists and camera operators burst into laughter. "No. Zero." He was most emphatic. "I have no such power. But I *hope* that I have such power. Then, even before you ask the question . . . if I know the question, then it won't cause me any trouble." He couldn't restrain himself. He threw his head back and laughed long and hard, his expressive face contorted with mirth. One Czech reporter wiped tears of laughter from her eyes. Everyone in the room was starting to enjoy the press conference.

The woman looked down at the floor for a moment. She was clearly disappointed by the Dalai Lama's answer. But she was determined not to be deterred by the commotion. She pressed on: "My question is: Will you use e-mail occasionally

4

or do you still use telepatee?" She was obviously convinced that telepathy was part of the Dalai Lama's arsenal of esoteric skills.

The Dalai Lama turned to Tenzin Geyche Tethong, his private secretary, for help. They spoke briefly in Tibetan. The woman's face was flushed as she waited.

"Although His Holiness personally does not use the e-mail, all the Tibetan offices are already on the Internet," Tenzin Geyche explained in an even tone.

The Dalai Lama added something in Tibetan.

Tenzin Geyche continued: "As far as the computer is concerned, His Holiness finds it difficult even knowing where to press the button." In spite of himself—the private secretary usually kept his emotions under tight wraps in these public situations—he allowed himself a smile.

The Dalai Lama elaborated: "My fingers . . ." He put his hand up close to his face and stared at the splayed fingers. "Quite well, I think, quite suitable to use screwdriver." Now he made like a carpenter's tool with his right hand. The clicking of cameras went into high gear.

"Doing little something here and there . . ." The Dalai Lama continued as he peered raptly at his pirouetting fingers. "That at least I'm able. But for computer . . ." He clumsily punched the table a few times with his forefinger. "Hopeless."

As the press conference ended, journalists crowded around to shake the Dalai Lama's hand. The European woman was among them. He walked up to her, thrust his face inches from hers, and poked a finger firmly at her forehead. She shrieked. Her right hand shot out in a flash and grabbed his hand. The two of them laughed uproariously, without inhibition.

THESE DAYS, in the eyes of the world, the Dalai Lama has become an international icon. The fact that he is the leader of the Tibetan people, that he is the most recognizable symbol of Buddhism, is of less importance to the public. In the West, he comes across as part ascetic superstar and part cuddly panda bear. When he came to New York in 2003, he gave a four-day teaching to sellout crowds at the Beacon Theatre. The glittering marquee over the entrance proclaimed: On stage: the Dalai Lama. Coming soon: Twisted Sister and Hot Tuna.

The day after the teachings, the Dalai Lama gave a talk at Central Park. Under a brilliant sky, the East Meadow was blanketed with loyal fans, spiritual seekers, and the simply curious. An enormous stage, bracketed by two gigantic Videotrons, was erected for the occasion. Those who couldn't find space in the grassy fields had to peek through dense foliage from beyond the tree line. All told, 100,000 came for the event of the season. It was a mini-Woodstock choreographed by actor Richard Gere. Only Billy Graham and the Pope have drawn more people to Central Park.

The Dalai Lama was in good form that day. Standing just a few feet behind him, I could sense he was energized by the large crowd. As usual, he was self-deprecating, his humor gentle and his laugh hearty. Speaking without notes, he told his listeners, "Some of you come with certain expectations of Dalai Lama. The Nobel Peace laureate give some kind of exciting information or something special. Nothing! I have nothing to offer, just some blah, blah, blah."

But then he went on to reiterate a favorite theme: "We have to make every effort to promote human affection. While we oppose violence or war, we must show there is another way—a nonviolent way. Now look at humanity as a whole. Today's reality: whole world almost like one body. One thing happens some distant place, the repercussions reach your own place. Destruction of your neighbor as enemy is essentially destruction of yourself. Our future depends on global well-being."

Within a few minutes, he had the crowd's undivided attention.

A Tibetan photographer, obviously in awe of the Dalai Lama, whispered into my ear, "He doesn't need to read from the TelePrompTer. He is a living example of his wisdom—wisdom totally relevant to today's world."

I WAS CURIOUS if the Dalai Lama ever wondered why he is such a people magnet. In one of my interviews with him, I said, "I'd like to ask you a silly question." The Tibetan leader was sitting cross-legged, as usual, in his corner armchair in the audience room inside his residential compound in Dharamsala, India. "Why are you so popular? What makes you irresistible to so many people?"

The Dalai Lama sat very still, mulling the question over. He didn't brush my question aside with a joke, as I thought he might.

He was thoughtful as he replied. "I don't think myself have especially good qualities. Oh, maybe some small things. I have positive mind. Sometimes, of course, I get a little irritated. But in my heart, I never blame, never think bad things against anyone. I also try to consider others more. I believe others more important than me. Maybe people like me for my good heart.

"Now, I think at the beginning, they have curiosity. Then perhaps . . . usually when I meet someone for the first time, that someone not stranger to me. I always have impression: he another human being. Nothing special. Me too, same."

He rubbed his cheeks with his fingers and continued, "Under this skin, same nature, same kinds of desires and emotions. I usually try to give happy feeling to the other person. Eventually many people talking something positive about me. Then more people came, just follow reputation—that also possible."

The Dalai Lama has his own inimitable way with the English language. I had trouble understanding him when I first sat down to work on the book with him; he could be frustratingly cryptic at times. Eventually I got used to his manner of speaking and am now thoroughly entranced by its charm and directness.

"Sometimes when people come into contact with you," I said, "even without hearing you speak, just by watching you, they get emotional. Why?"

"I notice sometime, one singer or one actor," the Dalai Lama replied. "When they appear, some people almost like crying, jumping and crying. Similar." He bopped up and down on his chair and flapped his arms a few times.

"You're like a rock star," I said.

"Yes," the Dalai Lama said matter-of-factly. "But there may be other factors. We believe in other lifetimes in the past. So maybe some karmic link, something more mysterious." He frowned and looked into the distance. I had the impression he was trying to figure out for himself this more subtle explanation of his charisma.

He unwrapped his outer shawl and rearranged it around his torso.

Finally he said: "Now, this mysterious level. For example, some people get strange dream, then that dream open new future or new life or new connections with other people."

He pointed at me as he continued with his train of thought. "Your own case. Somehow, unexpectedly, something brought you here. That kidnap in Afghanistan. If that not happened, you may not be here. Then you may not develop all these connections with me and with the Tibetans. So all these, I'm certain they have causes and conditions. From Buddhist viewpoint: There may be karmic links in many past lives. Perhaps that's why many people feel close to me today."

Yes, "That kidnap in Afghanistan." In 1971, after finishing

college, I had bought a VW camper in Utrecht and planned to make my way overland from Holland to India. After traversing Turkey and Iran, I stopped and took a half-year break in Afghanistan—a haven then for dropouts and would-be adventurers.

It was near the end of that sojourn when I and two young women—Cheryl from New York and Rita from Munich—were abducted in Kabul by three Afghan men. Wielding one rifle between them, they forced us into a badly rusted car and drove us to a small village high up in the Hindu Kush. After several days of captivity, we managed to escape when their car skidded on a hairpin curve and crashed into the side of the mountain.

Soon after, Cheryl and I decided to travel together to India. She had a letter of introduction to the Dalai Lama, who lives in exile in Dharamsala. We headed directly to the picturesque Tibetan settlement. A few days after our arrival, we were granted an audience. On a crisp, overcast spring day in March 1972, I met the spiritual and temporal leader of the Tibetan people for the first time.

Fate. Karma. Whatever it is called. Yes, the Dalai Lama was right. If I had not been kidnapped, I certainly would not have met him then. Let alone collaborate on a book and ask him questions about his charisma.

Still pondering my question about his larger-than-life personality, the Dalai Lama continued, "Also, many people like my laugh. But what kind of laugh, what kind of smile, I don't know."

"Many people have commented on this laughter," I said, "this sense of play that you have. You're close to seventy, but you still love horseplay and you don't take yourself seriously."

"First, Tibetan people generally more jovial," the Dalai Lama said. "In spite of many difficulties, they usually ready to laugh, something like that. Then my family. All our brothers, except for Gyalo Thondup [his second oldest brother], like that," the Dalai Lama said. "Our eldest brother, [Thubten Jigme] Norbu, always make fun, always joke. My immediate brother, the late Lobsang Samten, very dirty jokes, great fun. And me. Then youngest brother, Tenzin Choegyal; younger sister, Jetsun Pema; also late eldest sister, all not serious. Our mother also. Our father also—short temper but very light heart.

"In my own case, my mental state, comparatively more peaceful. In spite of difficult situation or even sometimes very tragic sort of news, my mind not much disturbed. For a short moment, some sad feelings, but never remains long. Within a few minutes or a few hours, and then it goes. So I usually describe something like the ocean. On the surface, waves come and go, but underneath always remain calm."

People who come into contact with the Dalai Lama seem to sense that he is "for real," as Archbishop Desmond Tutu once said to me. And without exactly knowing why, they are affected by him, drawn to his larger-than-life humanity, even from a distance.

I have little doubt that the Dalai Lama's vigorous presence has something to do with his deep well of spirituality.

His legendary warmth is simply a manifestation of his spiritual attainment.

I've known the Dalai Lama for over three decades. He calls me his "old friend." During the last few years, I've been given unprecedented access to him while co-authoring this book. I've observed the Dalai Lama at close quarters, traveled with him as part of his entourage, and spent time with him at his home. But I find it difficult to describe, let alone pinpoint, his remarkable magnetism. To try to understand his essence, we have to look at his half-century-long Buddhist training and the singular way he relates to the world around him.

Much of his approach to life is fueled by a handful of fundamental but difficult-to-relate-to insights. On several occasions, he has told me something about interdependence and emptiness, two ideas that are of critical importance to him. I have listened carefully and taken notes. I must admit it was a struggle to understand these concepts. But by being his shadow, by being with him for hours on end, I came to identify some of the qualities that define him. The Dalai Lama's principles of compassion and nonviolence give shape to his global vision. And his unrelenting pursuit of forgiveness as a solution to conflict conditions the way he acts.

One thing I know for sure. I feel good around the Dalai Lama. I know people feel good around him. Perhaps we intuit that he walks the talk. We sense an uncommonly pure center inside him. Like a mirror reflecting light, it allows us to see and get in touch with our own humanity.

Desmond Tutu, his good friend of many years, had this to say about the Dalai Lama when they shared a stage in Vancouver, Canada, in front of a crowd of 14,000.

A few years ago, I was in San Francisco when a woman rushed up to greet me very warmly. She said to me, "Hello, Archbishop Mandela!" Sort of like getting two for the price of one.

I'm quite certain that no one is likely to make that mistake about His Holiness the Dalai Lama.

Isn't it extraordinary, in a culture that worships success, that it isn't the aggressively successful, the abrasive, the macho who are the ones that we admire. We might envy their bank balances, but we do not admire them.

Who are the people we admire? Well, there are many things you might say of a Mother Teresa, but macho is not one of them. All of us revere her for having been such a spendthrift on behalf of derelicts. We admire her because she is good. We admire people such as a Nelson Mandela for being an icon of magnanimity, of forgiveness, of reconciliation.

And we revere the Dalai Lama. He is about the only one, one of the very, very, very, very few, who can fill Central Park in New York with adoring devotees.

But why? Why? Because he is good, he is good, he is good. I have met very few other persons as holy as His Holiness. I have met very, very few who have his serenity, his deep pool of serenity.

And his sense of fun. He laughs easily; he is almost like a schoolboy with his mischievousness. Fun, fun, bubbling, bubbling joy.

And that's odd. That's odd for someone who has been in exile for forty-five years. By rights, he should be filled with resentment, with anger, with bitterness. And the last thing he should be wanting is to extend compassion and love to those who have treated him and his people so abominably. But he does. He does.

And aren't we all proud to be human? The Dalai Lama makes us feel good about being human. About being alive at a time when someone like him is around.

1.

Fu Manchu's Goatee

The alarm rang at 4:00 A.M. sharp. I turned it off with relief. I had bought the traveling clock the day before at the bazaar, and I had been worried about whether it would work properly. I'd had many frustrating experiences in the past with Indian-made timepieces.

I dressed hurriedly, grabbed my camera gear, and walked out of the backpackers' hotel. I could see the dark shapes of the Dhauladhar range, the Outer Himalayas, rising above the small hill station of Dharamsala. It was very quiet; it would be a couple of hours before the town stirred itself. There was not a soul in sight. I walked quickly past the small, empty bus square, then broke into a run along the winding road leading to the Dalai Lama's residence.

Tenzin Taklha, the Dalai Lama's deputy private secretary,

was waiting for me by the palace gate. Wearing a short-sleeved shirt and long gray pants, he looked rested and relaxed at this early hour. I was flustered, my damp shirt stuck uncomfortably to my back despite the cool temperature.

"I'm sorry you had to get up this early," I apologized.

"It's no problem. I seldom get to be with His Holiness when he meditates early in the morning. It's a rare privilege for me," Tenzin, a handsome man in his thirties, replied with a slight smile.

I had begun interviewing the Tibetan leader for our book project a year earlier, in 1999. But this was the first time I was given permission to be with him this early in the morning.

Even at this hour, several Indian soldiers and a couple of Tibetan security guards were milling about the entrance. Tenzin led me directly through the big metal gates. I was surprised. Although I was by now a well-known figure—within the past year, I had interviewed the Dalai Lama half a dozen times—I always had to walk through a set of metal detectors and then be patted down thoroughly by a Tibetan bodyguard. Every visitor went through this routine; there was no exception.

I seemed to have crossed an invisible line this morning. At least for now, I belonged to a handful of non-Tibetans who were trusted confidants of the Dalai Lama. I would be allowed to enter the Dalai Lama's private quarters without being checked for concealed weapons.

My mind went back to another occasion when I'd walked through these same gates in March 1972. Back then, there was only the lone Indian sentry manning the entrance. I'll always treasure the memory of that spring day when I met the Dalai Lama for the first time. I was twenty-seven.

Dressing carefully for that meeting more than thirty years ago, I had pulled on a pair of snug-fitting black velvet trousers. The seat was a touch problematic; it was so worn that you could see through the material. My black cotton shirt, bought in Kabul, was soft and light, its cuffs trimmed with narrow bands of hand-stitched embroidery. The pièce de résistance, however, was the hooded black cape I had bought in Marrakech. I was very attached to it, and unless it was really hot, I always had it draped around me, Zorro-style.

The all-black ensemble went well with my Fu Manchu goatee, I thought. I had patiently nurtured it over the last couple of years as I traveled through Europe and Asia. But I was starting to get frustrated with it. It was thin and wispy, not quite the luxuriant growth I had had in mind. And another thing: it had a tendency to curve inward toward my Adam's apple. Despite my daily ministrations—pulling it frequently to encourage it to conform to gravity—all it wanted to do was hide.

My hair was shiny and long, nearly level with the small of my back. I gave it a good comb-through and tied it into a ponytail. With my best clothes on, the flowing cape hiding the bald spot on the back of my pants, I was ready for my audience with the so-called God-King of Tibet.

I knew very little about the Dalai Lama and his country. I had spent the first twenty years of my life in Hong Kong.

Tibet was most emphatically not in the school syllabus of the Crown Colony. The attention of my Chinese school-mates was focused squarely on the West, on its great business and medical schools and its glorious technological advances. The frozen, forbidding tract of land known as the Roof of the World was not someplace that piqued their imagination.

I was no different, but for one thing. In high school I devoured the books of Jin Yong, the greatest storyteller I had ever known in my young life. The Tibet of my imagination was shaped by Jin Yong's febrile mind. It was in his kung-fu novels that I first learned of enigmatic Tibetan lamas who had developed supernatural powers after meditating for years in their mountaintop hermitages. This romantic image of Tibetan monks, embodiment of spirituality and physical prowess, had stayed in my consciousness.

Cheryl Crosby, a Buddhist from New York, was the reason I got to meet the Dalai Lama. A friend of hers, Dorje Yuthok, the matriarch of an aristocratic Lhasa family, had written her a letter of introduction to the Tibetan leader. Cheryl was only a few years older than I, but there was a large gap in maturity between us. She was self-assured and made friends easily. Even while we were kidnapped in Kabul, she had the presence of mind to keep up a semblance of patter with our captors. After our escape, we had traveled together to Dharamsala.

There I met my first Tibetans. I saw men and women walking around the narrow streets, twirling prayer wheels; many still wore traditional robes and colorful knee-high felt boots. I drank in their kind, unguarded faces. There was genuine warmth in them. They smiled easily and often. There was always an undercurrent of play, of gaiety in every encounter. There was no doubt about it. Dharamsala, also known as Little Lhasa, was the mellowest place I'd ever been.

On the afternoon of the audience, Cheryl and I followed a middle-aged Tibetan attendant through the palace gates. An Indian soldier inside the grounds was leaning on his rifle, smoking a bidi. He barely looked at us as we walked up the short driveway to the audience hall. That was the extent of security around the Dalai Lama in those days.

The audience room, painted a rich shade of yellow, was spacious and bright. Tibetan painted scrolls hung on the walls. We sat down on plain but comfortable Indian-made armchairs and waited. I was keyed up by the prospect of meeting someone who was regarded by many as both a god and a king. But that excitement was tinged with some apprehension. Though there was much about Tibet that I didn't know, I knew this much: the Chinese had invaded the Dalai Lama's country in the fifties, killed a great many of his subjects, and forced him to take refuge in India. By all accounts, the Chinese treatment of the Tibetans during the occupation was horrific. And I, of pure Yellow Emperor stock, was about to come face-to-face with the supreme leader of the Tibetans. It was unlikely that the Dalai Lama had met many Chinese after his exile in 1959. I was worried that he might be hostile.

As I mulled over the possible scenarios, two young monks dressed in identical maroon robes walked in. I recognized the Dalai Lama immediately. He was thirty-seven. But with his glasses and unlined face, he looked remarkably youthful. Unlike many of his countrymen, he was pale and his features delicate. His gentle, unassuming demeanor was another revelation. He was slight, to the point of being skinny. So was the monk next to him, who was considerably shorter. I later found out that his name was Tenzin Geyche Tethong, the scion of a well-known Lhasa family and the Dalai Lama's translator and private secretary.

As he was about to sit down, the Dalai Lama glanced over at us. He took me in for the first time. He stared at my goatee and started to giggle. Not the deep baritone rumble that I have come to know so well. It was a high-pitched giggle that went on for some time. He had trouble controlling himself, and he was bending forward with the effort. Meanwhile, Cheryl had started her full-body prostrations. She was startled by the unexpected giggles, but she was determined to finish.

I stood there that March afternoon, feeling awkward. I didn't know what I was supposed to do. I didn't know how to prostrate. Anyway, I didn't feel like kowtowing to this young man in the throes of bursting his guts over my appearance.

The Dalai Lama finally got a grip on himself. He smiled sheepishly at Cheryl as she presented a *khata*, a white offering scarf. I unfolded mine and approached him. He stole another glance at me, and the giggles started again. Even solemn-looking Tenzin Geyche was grinning broadly now.

The next half hour was a blur. I have no recollection of how the conversation began. I vaguely remember Cheryl telling him about herself, that she practiced Tibetan Buddhism, and that she was a friend of Mrs. Dorje Yuthok in New York. Cheryl had a few questions for the Dalai Lama, mostly about her practice of Buddhism. I have long since forgotten what she wanted to know and what his responses were. Tenzin Geyche carefully translated. In those days, the Dalai Lama's English was a notch below the pidgin English spoken by many Indians. He would have been lost without his translator. From time to time, however, he ventured a few simple English phrases.

Then the Dalai Lama turned and faced me. I had been racking my brain to come up with some clever questions. But I knew little about Tibet and even less about Tibetan Buddhism. So I asked him something that had gnawed at me since I first walked through the doors of the audience room.

I asked him if he hated the Chinese.

The Dalai Lama seemed subdued in his interchange with Cheryl. Now he straightened up in his chair. His reply was immediate and succinct. And it was in English.

"No," he said.

His eyes held mine. His expression was solemn. There was no hint of gaiety left. I looked away and stared at the carpeted floor.

After an interminable silence, he spoke quietly and slowly to Tenzin Geyche in Tibetan.

The private secretary translated: "His Holiness does not have any bad feelings toward the Chinese. We Tibetans have suffered greatly because of the Chinese invasion. And as we speak, the Chinese are systematically, stone by stone, dismantling the great monasteries of Tibet. Nearly every Tibetan family in Dharamsala had a sad story to tell; most have lost at least one family member due to Chinese atrocities. But His Holiness said his quarrel is with the Chinese Communist Party. Not with ordinary Chinese. He still considers the Chinese his brothers and sisters. His Holiness doesn't hate the Chinese. As a matter of fact, he forgives them with no reservations."

It is amazing how clearly I remember that snippet of the conversation three decades later. Maybe it is because the answer was so unexpected, so unlike the picture Jin Yong had painted with his stories. Every one of his tales has revenge as a recurring theme. A man's honor is defined by the heroic and simple credo: an eye for an eye—much like the samurai code of feudal Japan. I marveled at the idea that the Dalai Lama forgave the Chinese for what they had done to his people.

Cheryl had been weeping quietly, overwhelmed by the audience. As we prepared to leave, the Dalai Lama walked over and consoled her; then he shook hands gravely with me.

I left the audience room relatively unmoved. I had expected a king, but he was one of the most un-king-like people I'd ever met. Although friendly enough, he was too down-to-earth, a touch too humble. There was little saintly aura about him, and he giggled too much.

Later, as I continued my travels eastward to Burma, Hong Kong, and then the United States, I would come to regard the short time I had spent in Dharamsala as *the* peak experience of my travels around the world. The Tibetans there had made an indelible impression on me.

For more than a decade after that 1972 audience with the Dalai Lama, things Tibetan still loomed large in my mind. They also fired up my dormant nomadic instincts. From 1984 on, using Kathmandu as a base, I roamed the wide, open spaces of Tibet for four years to research a guidebook about its pristine pilgrimage sites.

The landscape of the high plateau was poignant and stunning, unlike any I had seen in all my earlier years of wandering. The Tibetans were as I remembered them in Dharamsala: gentle, generous, and prone to sudden belly laughs. The fact that I'm an ethnic Chinese did not stop them from being helpful to me.

And the smiling visage of the Dalai Lama was never far away. All the village houses and monasteries I visited had his photograph on the altar. Every Tibetan I met asked about him, often with tears in their eyes. All of a sudden, the Dalai Lama and what he stood for took on more significance in my mind. It struck me that he and his countrymen practice a very simple religion—they practice being kind to one another.

As the metal gates of the Dalai Lama's residence closed behind us, Tenzin Taklha and I walked up the wide concrete path to the audience-hall complex, where my interviews with the Tibetan leader always took place. We bypassed the complex and a small chanting hall and then walked through a heavily wooded area. Beyond were the gardens and the handsome two-story building where the Dalai Lama sleeps and meditates. This was the farthest I had ever gone into the compound.

An Indian soldier cradling an automatic weapon patrolled the area outside the entrance. Another Indian, a man in plainclothes with white shirttails hanging outside his trousers, watched us impassively. Three or four Tibetan bodyguards paced in silence. As we stood in front of the house, I felt awkward, an interloper in the innermost sanctum of the Dalai Lama.

As if on cue, the Tibetan leader walked out of the building, peered at me, smiled, and said, *"Ni hao?"* in his booming baritone. He loves to use the Chinese greeting with me. Giving my hand a good squeeze, he started up the path through the gardens. He marched briskly along the gentle incline for about fifty yards and then turned back. He was chortling as he came toward me; he was showing off. We had talked about the importance of exercise a few months earlier. At the time, he confessed to me that he didn't like physical exercise, that he was terribly lazy about it. I got him to promise he would increase his quota, from thirty full-body prostrations a day to a hundred. Now he was eager to show me how seriously he took his morning exercise.

He gestured for Tenzin and me to follow him. We walked up a flight of concrete exterior stairs to the brightly lit second floor—a large, open space with a few comfortable sofas and armchairs scattered about. Oriental rugs covered sections of the parquet floor, and floor-to-ceiling windows took up the entire right wall. I could see the Kangra Valley falling sharply away, the tips of the mountains mellowing with first light.

Then the Dalai Lama led us into his meditation room.

2.

Two Monks on the Parapet

The Dalai Lama's meditation room was bathed in soft, early-morning light. Meticulously crafted wood cabinets lined the walls; within them I could see numerous bronze statues and myriad religious artifacts. Stacks of Tibetan scriptures wrapped in yellow cloth and rich brocades were piled neatly on custom-made shelves. The center of the room was dominated by an ornate altar. A statue—no more than a couple of feet tall, enclosed in a miniature glass-and-wood temple—had pride of place. The space was serenely gorgeous, its elegance understated.

Tenzin Taklha motioned for me to sit near the entrance on a little square Tibetan carpet. I set up my camcorder on a tripod. Without a word, the Dalai Lama went behind his simple mahogany desk. He slipped off his plastic flip-flops and sat down in the lotus position, his back against the wood-paneled wall. He adjusted his robes about him, closed his eyes, and began to meditate. I started the camera and heard the faint whir of the motor as it captured the Tibetan monk on digital tape.

The Dalai Lama had told me something about his morning routine: "As soon as I wake up, these days exactly 3:30, I recite some mantras or some prayers. My first thoughts: Buddha and his teaching of compassion, teaching of interdependence. That I always do—the rest of my day guided according to these two things: altruism and interdependence. Then some prostrations. I think altogether doing prostrations and some exercise, about thirty minutes. I always take a bath, shower, after. Then around 5:00 or sometimes 4:40 my breakfast. My younger brother always tease me: the real purpose of rising up early is for breakfast. Usually, as a Buddhist monk, no evening meal."

As the Dalai Lama settled into his meditation, my eyes adjusted to the subdued lighting. Directly across the room from me was a wall mural framed within a glass-and-wood cabinet. It showed the figure of a Buddha dressed in simple ocher robes; in the background were lush green mountains and meandering inlets. The Buddha's head conformed to traditional proportions, with its long earlobes and topknot signifying enlightenment. He had an indeterminate look—halfway between smiling and repose. His entire face—the slightly chubby cheeks, the small chin, the corners of his eyes—was pregnant with incipient mirth.

The Dalai Lama's meditation had clearly gotten into some kind of deep inner state very quickly. Nothing existed outside of him—not the room, not Tenzin and me sitting no more than a few feet away. His meditation style is different from that, say, of a Zen master. Like many Tibetan lamas, he doesn't sit rock-still and rigid. There are always slight movements. He sways from side to side; he stops and is completely immobile for a while; then comes a short mantra, muttered under his breath, a hand reaching around to the back of his neck to scratch an eczema itch. If I hadn't seen him in deep meditation before, I would have sworn he was fidgeting.

All of a sudden, his eyes rolled back in their sockets and his half-opened eyelids fluttered involuntarily. The intimacy of the movement was unnerving.

The Dalai Lama's desk was cluttered. On it were his scriptures—stacks of unbound Buddhist canons, a clear glass vase of cut flowers, a multi-levered desk lamp, and a small bronze Buddha. There was also a high-end Swiss Army knife, crammed with every conceivable contraption, placed next to a desk clock with a tiny figurine on top. To his left was a knee-high wooden cabinet topped with a red paper organizer. Another cabinet, of similar height, formed the right wall of the small alcove. Piled on top were books, more Tibetan scriptures, three containers filled with pens and highlighters, and a bottle of protein supplement. Towering over these odds and ends was a luxuriant bouquet of yellow and red silk flowers—mostly lilies and roses—overflowing from a slate-gray vase. They looked amazingly real, down to the tiny dew-drops clinging to the petals. A TV remote was close by.

The meditation room was the Dalai Lama's private sanc-tuary, a place for contemplation as well as for work. It was the one place where he could be truly alone—he confers with of-ficials and greets visitors within the audience complex near the entrance of the residential compound. It was here, in this room, that he marshaled his inner resources—through med-itation, through rereading the words of ancient Tibetan mas-ters—to come up with the requisite wisdom to guide himself and his people through difficult times.

The Dalai Lama took off his glasses when he meditated, and that was how I first became acutely conscious of his age. I could see the deep pouches beneath his eyes, the vertical ridges that ran from under his cheekbones all the way down to his chin. The Tibetan leader was then in his mid-sixties.

It gives me pleasure to look at the Dalai Lama's face. It is such a contrast to mine. His is full of wrinkles; each one tells a tale of struggle, suffering, or joy. Although I'm only ten years younger, my face is relatively smooth, the wrinkles still tentative. My face has often been a source of quiet exasper-ation to me. Not that it is ugly or offensive; it is an average, ordinary face. But it is one that seems always to be in repose. It is not a face that anyone would call animated.

I grew up in a traditional Chinese family. Overt displays of emotions were discouraged. There were the odd moments when I showed unalloyed joy—as when I received a packet of *laisi*, a red envelope containing a tidy stack of dollar bills, from my Ninth Uncle at New Year's. I had a big grin plastered on my face then. And I was also capable of showing intense anger—as when my little sister threw my favorite kung-fu novel out the window. But I cultivated a neutral face most of the time. I was unusually self-conscious, and my guard was continually up. Perhaps that's why I was such a good poker player at college.

Keeping my face neutral suited me well enough for most of my life. But in recent years, I've discovered I paid a price for that. Over time, my ability to experience emotions became impaired. This was most noticeable when my mother died. I found I had to consciously summon up feelings of sadness at her funeral. I had become the quintessential inscrutable Asian.

The Dalai Lama, however, wears his soul on his face. Many people have noticed this about him, including Paul Ekman, a professor of psychology and the world expert on facial expressions.

Ekman is a connoisseur of the human face. He has studied it in minute detail for the last four decades. In his research, Ekman has catalogued the facial muscles and studied how they twitch and tug to generate some 7,000 different expressions. He has correlated the most meaningful of these to what they signify emotionally. In the process, he has become a human lie detector par excellence. Following the bombing of the World Trade Center on September 11, 2001, a CIA-FBI counterterrorism task force hired Ekman as a consultant on how to detect lies when questioning suspects. One of the things he taught agents to look for was very subtle expressions—a slight movement of an inner eyebrow muscle called frontalis pars medalis, for example, is an indication of sadness.

Ekman first met the Dalai Lama in March 2000 in Dharamsala, at the Eighth Mind and Life Conference between Buddhists and Western scientists. The theme of the conference was Destructive Emotions. Over the course of five intensive days, the psychologist had plenty of opportunities to observe the Tibetan leader. Ekman marveled that in all his years of studying faces, he had never seen one like the Dalai Lama's. His facial muscles were vital and supple; they seemed to belong to someone in his twenties.

Why this extraordinary discrepancy? Ekman thought he knew the answer: the Dalai Lama uses his facial muscles more vigorously than anyone Ekman has ever known. And there is precision in the way the Dalai Lama expresses himself; there are seldom any mixed signals. When he is happy, he is one hundred percent happy. No other sentiments creep in to adulterate the sensation.

Ekman was impressed with the Dalai Lama's face for another reason. With the possible exception of some young children, the Tibetan leader's face was the most guileless one encountered by Ekman in all his decades of research. And like these children, the Dalai Lama was totally at ease with displaying his emotions. He was not ashamed of his feelings; he saw no reason to be self-conscious or embarrassed about them. During the conference, an observer from California told the Dalai Lama that a young child in Dharamsala had died after being attacked by a rabid dog. Everyone present clearly saw the deeply felt grief on the Tibetan's face. This was a revelation to Ekman. He had no doubt that the Dalai Lama felt the loss as keenly as if his own child had been involved. But Ekman was also amazed that this expression of sorrow lasted for only a short time. Within a few moments, all echoes of grief had disappeared. Similarly, the Dalai Lama would laugh without restraint at something funny and then, within seconds, display the most serious concentration. He doesn't get too attached to things—including his own emotions.

WATCHING THE DALAI LAMA meditate, I managed to sit in a crude approximation of the lotus position for all of five minutes before the pain became too much. I shifted to a kneeling position and started to fiddle with the camcorder, panning first along one wall, taking in the ancient Tibetan painted scrolls and the exquisite statues, then back to the Dalai Lama. There was no way I could sit still like he did. The profound serenity of the room did nothing for me. Despite the powerful waves of meditative bliss no doubt radiating from the Dalai Lama, all I could think of was the in-flamed tendon connecting my right thigh to my right hip.

Then something caught my eye. On the other side of the room, half hidden between some small bronzes and a vase of freshly cut flowers, was a photograph in a small, dark green frame. It looked to be the only photo in the room, among the scores of *tankas*, objets d'art, and ancient scriptures.

And not only that—it was my photo. Or, rather, it had been my photo until I gave it to the Dalai Lama during our interview a few months earlier. I had taken the picture in Tibet in 1985. It shows two monks in red robes leaning halfway over a parapet on the roof of a monastery, engrossed in something happening below. The picture was taken from behind, so only the backs of their bodies can be seen. They are leaning so far off the parapet that it seems they might topple over at any moment. In front of them is a range of low hills.

It is a gorgeous picture: the rich, sumptuous red of the robes is so vivid that you can imagine touching and smelling the woolen cloth. Then there is the light brown, mottled moonscape of the high Tibetan plateau, the rounded hills lightly dusted with a thin coating of fresh, blue-tinted snow that brings all the nooks and crevices into sharp relief. At the right edge of the photo is a clump of tall, dark green trees, the celebrated and very sacred junipers of Reting Monastery.

Of the thousands of transparencies I took during the mid-eighties, as I sought out and documented Tibet's sacred places, that picture is my favorite. I'm not sure why that is so. There are many images that might strike a more powerful chord in the casual observer. And there are a few that would be better candidates for a *National Geographic* spread on Tibet. But for nearly two decades, that photo had been the one I kept at my bedside. Perhaps it was the way the two monks draped themselves ever so casually over the parapet. The childlike, carefree spontaneity of Tibetans is so different from the way I relate to people and things.

When I'd given the framed picture to the Dalai Lama, he had not been overly impressed. He gave the photo a cursory look, then handed it to Tenzin Taklha. He gets many gifts, and he almost always passes them along to his staff for safe-keeping. He appreciates the gesture, but he is simply not very focused on objects, beautiful or not.

Then, as an afterthought, the Dalai Lama had asked me, "What is this place?"

"It's the Reting Monastery, Your Holiness," I replied.

"Reting!" he said. "I went there in 1956."

He snatched the photo back from a startled Tenzin and peered closely at it.

"Reting. I remember it well. I felt a special closeness to it."

"Of the many pictures I took of Tibet, this is the one that I have always kept near me," I said.

"Well, we both have special feeling with Reting," the Dalai Lama said. "I was very moved when I was there. For some un-known reason, I felt very connected with the place. Since then, I have often thought of building a hermitage at Reting and spending the rest of my life there."

I had assumed at the time that the photo would be stored in some large repository of treasures in the residence, jostling for space with all the wondrous gifts and mementos the Dalai Lama had received over the years. So I was flabbergasted to see my photo here.

Tenzin noticed me staring at the photograph. He gave me a big grin. His hands were in his lap, but I saw that one thumb was up.

Yes, I was touched and more than a little proud that my photo was in the meditation room, so close to the Dalai Lama. I wanted to believe that he kept it there because he had a soft spot for me. But I knew, more likely than not, it was there because Reting Monastery claimed a special place in his heart.

It was getting lighter outside; the birds began to chirp. I could see the mist thinning a little down the Kangra Valley.

"Is that enough?" the Dalai Lama asked me, his early-morning meditation obviously finished for now.

"Yes, thank you, Your Holiness," I replied. What else could I say? I'd like to spend the whole day with you?

He got up from behind his desk. Tenzin and I scrambled to stand.

The Dalai Lama walked over to the wall mural and began rummaging among the small bronzes and butter lamps arrayed on the supporting ledge. Then he looked over his shoulder and said to me, "Come here."

He handed me a small replica of an Indian-style monastery. Made of gray stone, it was about three inches tall. It was meticulously carved: a five-story central tower sat on the roof of a two-story structure; four smaller towers anchored the four corners. The craftsman had carefully chiseled in tiny windows, doors, and other details on each floor. For such a small object, it was surprisingly heavy.

"Temple in Bodhgaya. For you," he said. Bodhgaya—the place where the Buddha reached enlightenment—is the supreme pilgrimage site for Buddhists.

Then the Dalai Lama handed me a second thing—a semi-precious stone, the size of a large marble, mounted in bronze. The stone had several gradations of brown, and a white stripe ran across its center. I had no idea what kind of stone it was. The Dalai Lama did not elaborate.

I was surprised at the gifts. Except for the obligatory khata—the traditional white scarf offering—I had never received gifts from him. Since these two objects were in the Dalai Lama's meditation room, I assumed they must hold special significance for him.

The Dalai Lama took my hand gently in his and led me to the door. Then he turned abruptly to a display case containing more bronzes and other marvelous-looking objects. He dug around in it, looking for something.

"Aha!" A look of delight on his face, he held up a small statue, a mahogany-colored image of an old man with a waist-length beard. It had a large face—distinct Asian features, with a strong nose and bushy eyebrows. In its right hand was a staff. It was a carving of a Chinese sage.

"For you. See you soon," the Dalai Lama said.

BACK AT MY HOTEL, I hummed a few bars of "A Whiter Shade of Pale" as I went through my day pack. My room door was open, and I could see a Tibetan woman drying clothes on the rooftop below the hotel. She too was humming a tune, though she was too far away for me to make it out. I took out my video gear to take a look at the morning footage. I turned on the camcorder and rewound the tape to the beginning. The first images on the small LCD screen were of the Dalai Lama sitting behind his desk in his meditation room. He was getting ready to start his meditation. The lighting was adequate and the sound was good. Suddenly, horizontal stripes leaped across the screen. Instead of the wall mural, there was nothing but semitransparent bars in differing shades of gray. The Dalai Lama had disappeared from the screen entirely.

I jabbed the fast-forward button. The stripes jiggled and danced. I stopped the tape and then pressed play. Stripes. Nothing but stripes. I rewound the tape to the beginning and played back the first frames. The colors were murky because of the low light, but the images of the Dalai Lama about to get into the lotus position were sharp. The following meditation footage had been obliterated. I rewound and played the tape over and over again until the battery started to run out.

3.

The Man from Derry

I had arrived early for my interview with the Dalai Lama in his audience hall in Dharamsala. The good-sized room, pleasantly cluttered with large Indian-style armchairs and couches, had a nice balance of natural and artificial light. Brilliant daylight, partially filtered by clumps of purple bougainvillea and greenery on the outside porch, bathed the room through large banks of windows. Eight colorful Tibetan hanging scrolls, each a representation of an aspect of the goddess Tara, hung near the ceiling.

But my eyes were drawn to something incongruous in the room. On a windowsill near the entrance, as if placed there in afterthought, was a solid crystal sculpture of the Capitol Building in Washington, D.C. Little more than a foot and a half tall, it was a hefty-looking object. I walked over to take a closer look. There was an inscription at the bottom. It was the First Annual Raoul Wallenberg Congressional Human Rights Award, presented to the Dalai Lama by the U.S. Congressman Tom Lantos.

The prize, named for the Swedish diplomat who saved thousands of Jews from Nazi death camps, was conferred on July 21, 1989. Less than three months later, on October 5, the Norwegian Nobel Committee announced in Oslo that the Tibetan had also won the Nobel Peace Prize. It cited the Dalai Lama's consistent opposition to violence and his advocacy of "peaceful solutions based upon tolerance and mutual respect in order to preserve the historical and cultural heritage of his people."

The Dalai Lama, then fifty-four, was the first Asian to be awarded the peace prize without having to share it. During the announcement, Nobel Committee Chairman Egil Aarvik admitted to reporters that nonviolence had not been successful in achieving independence for Tibet over the past three decades. But he believed there were no other honorable solutions. "Of course you may say it's a bit too unrealistic," he said of nonviolence. "But if you look at the world today, what is the solution to conflict? Will violence or military power be the solution? No . . . the path of peace is realistic. That is why the Dalai Lama has been chosen—because he is a very clear and outstanding spokesman for this peace philosophy."

At the heart of the Dalai Lama's peace philosophy is his ability to cultivate forgiveness. When I first met the Dalai Lama some three decades ago, he told me that he had forgiven the Chinese for what they have done to the Tibetans. At the time, I had been surprised. Now I wanted to learn more in the upcoming interview. As the Dalai Lama came into the audience hall and sat down across from me, I asked him without any preamble, "Your Holiness, I thought it natural that you'd harbor resentment toward the Chinese. Yet you've told me that this is not so. But do you, sometimes at least, experience deep feelings of animosity?"

"That almost never," the Dalai Lama replied. "I analyze like this: if I develop bad feelings toward those who make me suffer, this will only destroy my own peace of mind. But if I forgive, my mind becomes calm. Now, concerning our struggle for freedom, if we do it without anger, without hatred, but with true forgiveness, we can carry that struggle even more effectively. Struggle with calm mind, with compassion. Through analytical meditation, I now have full conviction that destructive emotions like hatred is no use. Nowadays, anger, hatred, they don't come. But little irritation sometimes come."

Whenever the Dalai Lama talks about forgiveness, he likes to use as an example the story of Lopon-la, a Lhasa monk he knew before the Chinese occupation.

"After I escaped from Tibet, Lopon-la put in prison by Chinese," the Dalai Lama told me. "He stayed there eighteen years. When he finally free, he came to India. For twenty years, I did not see him. But he seemed the same. Of course looked older. But physically OK. His mind still sharp after so many years in prison. He was still same gentle monk.

"He told me the Chinese forced him to denounce his religion. They tortured him many times in prison. I asked him whether he was ever afraid. Lopon-la then told me: 'Yes, there was one thing I was afraid of. I was afraid I may lose compassion for the Chinese.'

"I was very moved by this, and also very inspired."

The Dalai Lama paused. He tugged on his maroon robes and wrapped them tightly around him.

"Now. Lopon-la. Forgiveness helped him in prison. Because of forgiveness, his bad experience with Chinese not got worse. Mentally and emotionally, he didn't suffer too much. He knew he could not escape. So, better to accept reality than to be traumatized by it."

The Dalai Lama is convinced that Lopon-la's power of forgiveness helped him survive all those years in prison without irreparable damage to his psyche. On one of my European trips with the Dalai Lama, I met a man whose life, like Lopon-la's, was enhanced by forgiveness.

THE EUROPA OF BELFAST is the most bombed hotel in Europe, according to my copy of Lonely Planet guide to the U.K. It was bombed thirty-two times during the height of the Troubles, the three-decade-long fratricide between Catholics and Protestants in Northern Ireland. Since the hotel installed shatterproof windows in 1993, the bombings have dropped off.

After having breakfast in the elegant restaurant off the

Europa's marble lobby, I walked the few blocks to the glittering Waterfront Hall. Circular in shape, the brand-new glass-and-granite structure bore a striking resemblance to the starship *Enterprise*. The $52-million concert hall is a symbol of hope and regeneration for troubled Belfast. And, like the Guggenheim Museum in Bilbao, it has firmly put the city on the cultural map of Europe.

I was in the Waterfront Hall to meet up with the Dalai Lama. This was the Tibetan leader's first visit to Belfast. He was there to take part in an interfaith peace conference organized by Father Laurence Freeman, a Benedictine monk, and tour some of the trouble spots of Northern Ireland.

I caught up with the Dalai Lama in a reception room next to the lecture hall. He was standing next to Father Laurence and Seamus Mallon, the leader of Northern Ireland's Catholic faction. Mallon had a long white scarf wrapped around his neck, a gesture of friendship from the Tibetan. The Irishman was a bespectacled, white-haired man in his mid-sixties who looked older than his years. A central figure in Ireland's peace process, he hadn't taken a day off for years. He wanted to know how the Tibetan visitor liked his country.

"Very beautiful. And the people are . . ." The Dalai Lama fumbled for the right word. Tenzin Geyche Tethong made a stab: "warm." Tenzin Geyche, a short but distinguished-looking man, had served as consigliere to Tibet's supreme leader for most of his life. He had been a monk but had disrobed sometime ago.

"Yes, the people are very warm."

Then the Dalai Lama leaned toward Mallon, peering closely at him.

"But the wall between the people, the Catholics and the Protestants . . . that's bad. It's like a little Berlin Wall."

The "little Berlin Wall" is a five-meter concrete-and-metal structure topped with double rows of barbed wire, designed to keep the Catholics and Protestants from getting at one another's throats. Surveillance cameras are mounted at strategic intervals. The desolation around it is palpable: empty lots on both sides strewn with rubble, barbed wire, and decay. They call this wall, not far from Belfast's center, the Peace Line.

A block away is the Pony Club. Its walls still stood but the roof had caved in, the exposed beams charred by firebombs. It looked as though it had been this way for years. The area is a photojournalist's delight. Entire facades of the houses are painted with striking, colorful images culled from the Troubles. Most of them glorify the battle cry of the antagonists. Masked men in black outfits cradle machine guns. A four-story-high portrait of Bobby Sands—celebrated IRA hunger striker who in 1981 fasted himself to death over Britain's ruthless treatment of IRA prisoners—reads: our revenge will be the laughter of our children.

On the first day of his visit, the Dalai Lama came to the wall to plant a tree in Lanark Way. He got out of the car on the Protestant side; the street poles and curbs were daubed with blue, red, and white, the colors of the British Union

Jack (bombs painted in the tricolor had been tossed at Catholic houses one month earlier). A large crowd welcomed him, many of them children in school uniforms, waving multicolored Tibetan prayer flags. He waded into them, chatting and shaking hands.

Then the Dalai Lama walked up to the heavy steel gates. As the police, the Royal Ulster Constabulary, swung them open, a loud cheer went up from both sides of the wall. He slowly walked through the Peace Line to Catholic Springfield Road, where more children held up a large banner of welcome. The gates normally open only once a year—in July when the Protestant Orange Order march through them and up the Catholic side of the wall, an in-your-face show of chutzpah that ratchets up the ever-present tension in Belfast.

At the Peace Line, the Dalai Lama told the two warring communities that the best way to prevent conflict was by tempering emotions.

"When human emotions come out of control," he said to them, "then the best part of the brain in which we make judgments cannot function properly. Of course, some conflicts, some differences, will always be there. But we should use the differences in a positive way to try to get energy from different views. Try to minimize violence, not by force, but by awareness and respect. Through dialogue, taking others' interests and then sharing one's own, there is a way to solve the problems."

Tibet has suffered terribly under Chinese rule, so when the

Dalai Lama spoke to the crowd about the futility of violence, he spoke from a deep well of experience and pain.

"Isn't it incredible that people of the same Christian faith should fight with one another?" he said as he scanned the faces of Catholics and Protestants before him. "It seems foolish. I feel as if my head is spinning around from your problems. If somebody compared Buddhism and Christianity, then we have to think, yes, there are big differences. But between Protestants and Catholics? It's nothing! You and I have more differences than you do among yourselves. But I wish for you that you never lose hope. I can do nothing. The final outcome lies in the hands of the people of Northern Ireland."

At the end of his speech, the Dalai Lama asked the crowd, "Is that helpful?" A loud cheer went up. He then said, "If that's helpful, please remember it. If not, then"—he laughed— "then you forget it."

A Protestant minister and a Catholic priest flanked him on each side. He pulled the two men close together and hugged them. Then, with a mischievous glint in his eyes, he reached up and tugged their beards. The crowd was delighted. The Dalai Lama always has this thing about beards: he cannot resist playing with them.

The Belfast Telegraph published a cartoon in the editorial page about the visit: three thugs glowered at the smiling Dalai Lama as he was planting the sapling by the Peace Line; the leader snarled: "Yeah, but are you a Catholic Buddhist or a Protestant Buddhist?"

*T*HE NEXT AFTERNOON, the high sheriff of Belfast escorted the Dalai Lama into a well-appointed office in the City Hall, a Protestant stronghold known infamously as the Ulster Hall. The Dalai Lama slumped into a chair, his legs stretched all the way out. He was tired from his trip to Derry. He had gone there by private plane, after his early-morning session at the Waterfront Hall, to give a talk about forgiveness to thirty-four Catholics and Protestants, all victims of terrorist attacks that claimed 3,600 lives during the last thirty years.

During this brief fifteen-minute respite before the next event, the Dalai Lama had a chance to reflect on the Derry outing with Father Laurence, with whom he had been inseparable over the last couple of days due to their shared ideals and mutual respect.

Father Laurence, in his trademark white robes, was animated. If he was tired, he didn't allow it to show.

"You remember this young man in Derry, Richard Moore. He was blinded at the age of ten," Father Laurence prompted the Dalai Lama.

"By some shooting." The Dalai Lama came to life; he shifted in his chair and sat more upright. "But he's full of ideals, full of enthusiasm."

Father Laurence looked over to me.

"Imagine, His Holiness is a very joyful person, and this

THE WISDOM OF FORGIVENESS

man is very joyful, so they contributed equally to this meeting with the victims."

"One funny thing. You asked about . . ." The Dalai Lama trailed off and started to giggle. Then he rubbed his hand over his face.

Knowing exactly where the Dalai Lama was going, Father Laurence picked up the thread. "Richard didn't see blackness, so I asked him, 'What do you see?' He said, 'Well, I see people, like, I imagine them.' So I said, 'What does the Dalai Lama look like?' "

The Dalai Lama jumped in: "Then I let him touch my face." He wiped his face in a circular motion again with his hand. Then he grabbed his nose. "And my nose. And he said, 'Oh, big nose!' " The Dalai Lama clapped his hands together and burst into laughter, his body shaking with the effort.

Father Laurence continued, "Yes. Then you asked him how long it took to reconcile the trauma of losing his sight."

"And he replied, 'Overnight.' "

I had trouble relating to this little bit of information. If I had been in Richard Moore's shoes, my reaction would have been very different. I couldn't imagine getting over such a loss so quickly.

I talked to Richard Moore in Derry by phone a few months after the Dalai Lama's Northern Ireland visit. I was curious about his remarkable matter-of-fact acceptance of losing his sight.

"There were a couple of reasons why I accepted being

blind so quickly," he told me. "I had a lot of immediate support from family and friends. There was a lot of attention from the local and national media. Political leaders came to my house and fussed over me. Overnight I was a celebrity and I was made to feel important. Another thing. I was lucky: I was born a happy kid; I was given a happy, contented disposition."

"Were you ever depressed?" I asked.

"Two weeks out of the hospital," Moore replied, "my brother took me for a walk in the backyard. He asked me if I knew what happened. I said yes, I was shot. He asked me if I knew what damage was done. I said I didn't. He then told me that I'd lost one eye and I wouldn't be able to see with the other. I cried bitterly that night. I cried because I knew I wouldn't be able to see the faces of my daddy or mummy anymore. But that was it. The next day I accepted my fate.

"Of course, there have been deep, painful moments. I was there at the birth of my children, but I couldn't see them. They had their first communion. I would have given anything on earth to see them. Then there are all those Christmas mornings. . . . There is a price to pay and there always will be. But I don't allow that to dominate the rest of my life.

"My daddy always said: 'Never let one cloud ruin a sunny day.' "

I find it difficult to equate being shot in the eye to a passing cloud.

"How did you get shot?" I asked him.

"On May 4, 1972—I was ten years old—there was some trouble on the streets. I joined in and threw a rock at some British soldiers."

Moore was silent for a long moment.

He continued. "And then, well, I don't remember what happened next. A soldier shot a rubber bullet from nearby, and I was struck in the right eye. A teacher of mine was there but he didn't recognize me because my face was so disfigured. My daddy got into the ambulance with me. But he wouldn't let my mother come in; he didn't want my mother to see me. She had a brother shot dead in January 1972, on Bloody Sunday."

"What did you feel about the soldier who shot you?" I asked him.

"I know it's strange," Moore said, "but I felt no bitterness toward him—as a matter of fact, I would be quite intrigued to meet him. Let me tell you something. I think the biggest thing that helped me most in life was I held no grudges against him. I forgave him totally and without reservations."

Richard Moore's power of forgiveness led him into unsuspected directions in life. Some years ago, Moore started an organization called Children in Crossfire, which provides support to troubled children in Asia, Africa, and Latin America. Most recently he was in Bangladesh to help out with the program there.

I told Moore that the Dalai Lama was impressed with his resiliency, with what he had done with his life. I asked him what he thought of the Dalai Lama.

"After his talk in Derry that morning, I was invited to sit beside him at lunch," Moore said. "He served me himself. He piled curry beef and rice on my plate and then asked me if I had enough. He handed me my fork and knife. He showed me where my orange juice was. I could sense warmth coming from him, a strong, strong sense of love. Nothing you can put your finger on. I just felt relaxed and at home."

After lunch, while the Dalai Lama chatted with a radio journalist, Moore began to walk toward the Dalai Lama's car to wait for him to say good-bye.

"As I started up the driveway," Moore told me, "I heard the sound of running feet behind me. It was the Dalai Lama. He was running to catch up with me; he was out of breath. And he was shouting, 'Wait for your friend! Wait for your friend!' We then walked to the car together. He gave me a bear hug and was off."

AFTER HIS MEETING with the Irish victims in Derry, the Dalai Lama flew back to Belfast, where he gave a short talk about instilling harmony in the strife-torn Catholic-Protestant community. He was presented with a bouquet by Colin McCrory, a twelve-year-old boy with closely cropped hair. He grasped the boy's hands and shook them vigorously. At the end of the ceremonies, still high from the contact, Colin decided to walk back to his school, Hazelton Integrated, a Protestant school. Big mistake. He should have taken the bus with his friends instead. Along the way, he ran into a group of about ten teenagers who wanted to know what school he went to. After getting the truth from him, they threw him to the ground and repeatedly kicked him in the head. McCrory escaped serious injuries only when a woman ran over and broke up the lynching.

When Tenzin Geyche Tethong heard of the McCrory beating, he told the Dalai Lama right away. The Dalai Lama knew the Irish problem well. He was well briefed by Father Laurence, and one of his morning rituals in Dharamsala is to listen to the BBC World Service.

Still, he was unprepared to experience the sectarian hatred in so direct a manner. The twelve-year-old had just given flowers to him. They shook hands only hours ago. The Dalai Lama agonized over the viciousness of the attack, and he worried about the kid's head injuries. He had visited Budapest, Bratislava, and Prague just before coming to Belfast. The assault on young McCrory was the most disturbing incident he had encountered on the entire trip. It highlighted the intractability of the Irish problem as nothing else could.

4.

A Fire in the Navel

His Holiness was huddled with the archbishop. The Tibetan monk in his maroon robes and the Anglican priest in his black clergy suit sat with their heads almost touching, their hands clasped firmly together. They looked deep into each other's eyes, appearing for all the world like two love-struck teenagers. The world's media was kept at bay a few meters away, behind velvet restraining ropes. TV and print journalists from every continent were represented. It was not often that thirty-three Nobel Peace laureates were gathered in one room—the glittering banquet hall of Oslo's Holmenkollen Hotel. To celebrate one hundred years of the Nobel Peace Prize, Norway had assembled the biggest gathering of Nobel Peace laureates ever in December 2001.

The Dalai Lama and Archbishop Desmond Tutu were having a quiet private moment before the first morning session of the Nobel Centennial Symposium. I stood behind the two men, bent low, trying to catch the gist of their conversation above the clatter of camera shutters.

"I just came from northern Norway, where I received from Tromso University an honorary degree," the Dalai Lama was telling Archbishop Tutu. "One peculiar experience. One time I received another degree from Bologna University in Italy, the oldest university in Europe. There, there's one tradition. While I receive degree, besides put on beautiful clothes, also have to put on one ring. At that time, in front of the public, I mentioned, 'As a Buddhist monk I'm prohibited to wear ring, but today, because it's part of the ceremony, so I'll take.' I put on that ring for a short time."

"Yeah, very nice," Archbishop Tutu said. "And I'm sure you can sell the ring and raise a lot of money."

The two started to giggle—soft, giggly hee-hees at first. In no time, their giggles turned to loud guffaws and cackles. The Tibetan's a deep baritone; the other's high-pitched and squeaky. Their uninhibited and infectious laughter built to a cyclonic climax that shook the expansive French doors of the large hall. Everyone stopped what they were doing and stared.

I had a sudden flash. Despite the differences in skin color and age (Tutu is older by four years), the two men were identical twins in temperament. Each has the uncanny ability to throw himself totally into a situation and have unrestrained, spontaneous fun. Each is able to look at the most mundane things around him and manage to find something to laugh about.

One of the journalists stepped across the velvet rope and walked up to the two men, cameraman in tow.

She said to the Dalai Lama: "Can I ask you a question?"

"Where you're from?" he asked her, looking up.

"Norwegian TV. Your Holiness, what was most special for you in 2001?"

"I think the very shocking news, shocking experience," the Dalai Lama replied. "When I heard September eleventh, mainly when I saw the picture on TV, the civilian plane with innocent passengers—full of fuel and use as explosive weapon. Unthinkable. Also they plan, if not years, at least many months. I felt human intelligence guided or controlled by human hatred, disaster."

Archbishop Tutu nodded vigorously.

"So we have special responsibility to help promote positive human emotions, isn't it?" the Dalai Lama said to the archbishop.

"Very good, very good. Yes, I agree with you," Tutu said, clapping his hands.

*L*UNCH FOR THE LAUREATES and symposium guests at the Holmenkollen was a cloistered affair in the main restaurant. After the morning session, Archbishop Tutu and I entered the elegant room together. He knew that I was with the Dalai Lama and had graciously suggested I join him for lunch. We sat down at the table nearest the entrance. Almost immediately, we were joined by Colm O'Cuanachain, chairman of Amnesty International, the organization that had won the peace award in 1977. O'Cuanachain was followed closely by Cora Weiss, current head of the International Peace Bureau, winner of the Peace Prize in 1910. A waiter came by and asked us for our drink orders.

"Thank you, thank you very much," Archbishop Tutu said to him. "Now, I'm very hungry. Does that make a difference as to how quickly we get fed?"

"I can try to get a shortcut," the Norwegian waiter replied.

"Thank you, thank you." Archbishop Tutu exploded into another of his trademark guffaws.

I was nervous in such illustrious company. But I was determined to talk to the archbishop about his relationship with the Tibetan leader.

"What is your impression of the Dalai Lama?" I asked him, my voice unnaturally loud. O'Cuanachain and Weiss turned to look at me.

"He's a wonderful man. I love him," Tutu said right away. "Both of us have a tremendous sense of fun—inside us is a little child trying to get out. Jesus said: 'Unless you become as a little child, you'll not enter the kingdom of heaven.' The child has this sense of wonder, and so has the Dalai Lama. He also has this transparent holiness. He's got 'Holiness' as a title, but in fact, he is a holy man. Young people particularly find him irresistible. Young people are very quick to pick up on

when you're not authentic, when you're a dud. They realize
that the Dalai Lama's for real."

"You have this very special chemistry with the Dalai Lama,"
I continued. "When the two of you get together, it's like two
kids at play. How do you come by this special rapport?"

"I don't know, I don't know," Tutu said. "How do you fall
in love? It is something that just happens. There are people
who hit it off; you can't understand the alchemy. Why I hit
it off with him and he with me is just one of the glorious mys-
teries of . . . Let us say grace." He mumbled a quick prayer as
a bread basket arrived at the table.

"With your experience of apartheid, what can you say
about the Tibetans and the Chinese?" I asked the archbishop
as we munched on Norwegian rolls.

"One of the most important things: we black South
Africans believed fervently we'd win," Tutu replied. I could
sense that the other laureates at the table were hanging on to
his every word. "Belief, you know . . . sometimes you hold on
to it by the skin of your teeth. Especially in the dark days
when we were conducting funerals as if it was going out of
fashion. We were lucky: our people were extraordinary in
their capacity to laugh. They were able to laugh even in the
direst situations. They were even able to laugh at themselves.
Now, the Chinese. You know, they will ultimately lose. They
will also lose whatever regard the world has had for them.
The Chinese must remove this albatross around their necks
and allow the Tibetans to have real autonomy."

The waiter arrived with a big plate of fish and vegetables for Tutu. But nothing for the rest of us.

The archbishop's face lit up. "Well done, well done. God bless you. Very nice." To the table: "This man is very clever, very clever." As he exploded with laughter, his massive nostrils flared and his small eyes disappeared.

"Any moment now, for your friends. Any moment." The waiter was flustered by the unexpected paroxysm of merriment.

"I used a minute bitty-bit of influence—which we have in our hotline. I told him that my friends need also to benefit from the coziness we have here," Tutu explained to the rest of us, still laughing.

"We haven't benefited yet," O'Cuanachain said. I could hear his stomach growling.

"It's going to happen, it's going to happen," Tutu assured him, just before the waiter arrived with another tray of food.

*F*ROM 1995 TO 1997, Archbishop Tutu was chairman of South Africa's Truth and Reconciliation Commission. His job? To listen to 21,000 witnesses describe the human-rights abuses and atrocities committed during the apartheid era. At times, he wept openly after hearing the tales of torture, of people's limbs being blasted off with blowtorches. His mandate? He had to forgive the perpetrators in order to foster healing.

"People were saying," Tutu had said, "maybe we should

open the wounds, cleanse them so they don't fester. Pour balm on them. And then maybe, maybe, they would heal. Forgiveness is not cheap. And reconciliation is not easy. But with forgiveness, we open the door for someone. Someone who might have been shackled to the past, to break loose the shackles, walks back through the door and into a new future."

In 2004, Tutu, in a forum with the Dalai Lama at the University of British Columbia, talked about his experiences with the Commission.

Many times people were moved by examples, especially examples of people who, having suffered a great deal, instead of demanding a pound of flesh in retribution, have behaved extraordinarily.

A young black woman came to us and told this story: "The police came and took me to the police station. They put me in a room, undressed me. They took my breasts and they shove them into a drawer. And then they'd slam the drawer several times on my nipples until the white stuff oozed." Now, you imagine that someone who has experienced this kind of atrocity would be bitter, would lust for revenge. But frequently, people like her would say they were ready to forgive. We sat there and we were deeply, deeply humbled. Humbled by the privilege of listening to people who by right should have been angry, resentful, and vindictive. And instead, they were filled with a desire to forgive.

There was something called the Bisho massacre, thirty and forty people were killed and 200 injured. We held a public hearing in a huge hall, the room was packed to the rafters with angry people, many of whom were either injured at that incident or they had lost loved ones. Four officers that had shot and killed people came in. You could feel the tension in the room, the anger. They came and they sat over there on the stage and we were in the middle. One of the officers, a white officer, the other three were black, got up and said, "Yes, we gave the order for the soldiers to shoot."

The temperature shot up in the room, the tension you could cut with a knife. And then, he said, "Please forgive us. Please forgive these three of my colleagues and receive them back into the community." Now, you'd have thought this hall would erupt with anger. You know what that audience did? They applauded. Incredible. They applauded. And when the applause subsided, I said, "Let's keep a moment's silence. Because we are in the presence of something holy. We are standing on holy ground. We ought to be taking off our shoes, like Moses did."

Archbishop Tutu came by his deep-seated conviction of forgiveness through his exposure to an age-old piece of wisdom. As Tutu put it during his dialogue with the Dalai Lama in Vancouver: "In our country, we speak of something called *ubuuntu*. When I want to praise you, the highest praise I can give you is to say, you have ubuuntu—this person has what it takes to be a human being. This is a person who recognizes that he exists only because others exist: a person is a person through other persons. When we say you have ubuuntu, we mean you are gentle, you are compassionate, you are hospitable, you want to share, and you care about the welfare of others. This is because my humanity is caught up in your humanity. So when I dehumanize others, whether I like it or not, inexorably, I dehumanize myself. For we can only be human, we can only be free, together. To forgive is actually the best form of self-interest."

ONE MONTH after the Nobel laureates' gathering in Oslo, I sat down with the Dalai Lama in Dharamsala for an extended interview. During a discussion on the concept of forgiveness, the Dalai Lama told me the story of Lobsang Tenzin, a Tibetan Buddhist. By being truly forgiving, Tenzin's spiritual development had advanced dramatically.

"Tenzin was a freedom fighter in Tibet, in the Pempo area, one of the leaders of his village," the Dalai Lama began. "He was caught by the Chinese in 1959 and put in prison. Then he escaped to India. He did not know anything about Buddhism initially. But he somehow developed this practice of inner heat—*tumo*—by himself. He came to the practice quite late in life."

Tenzin had been meditating in a cave high above Dharamsala when he saw the intense light. It was the first sign that he was getting somewhere in his tantric practice. He closed his eyes to see if the light would disappear. It did not; it actually became more intense. Tenzin also had visions of a remarkable array of flowers. Then he felt a searing heat, like a fire with shooting sparks, in his navel area. By focusing his mind on it, he found that he could expand or contract the ball of fire and influence its movement. He moved it to his heart region, held it there, and meditated some more. There was a new sensation: he found that he was now immune to the biting cold. He was in awe of the experience, of his newfound ability to generate internal heat—tumo.

After continuing the meditation practice for about a year, Tenzin found that his meditation had reached another plateau: the psychic heat became more powerful, and its generation easier. Now he found that he could actually guide the heat energy into a central psychic channel in his body. Once this happened, he attained a state of bliss that was profound and long-lasting.

In the early 1980s, the Dalai Lama told Tenzin, then in his forties, that he should concentrate on tumo as a key component of his spiritual practice. At the Dalai Lama's suggestion, Tenzin sought out renowned tumo master Khyentse Lama of Manali, a small town high in the mountains of Himachal Pradesh, India.

"Khyentse Lama's disciples practiced tumo year-round, using the wet-sheet technique. Even on coldest days—nearly completely naked," the Dalai Lama told me. "Put sheet in ice water, then squeeze, then cover body and meditate. Within few minutes, steam comes. Completely dry in less than an hour. Again soak sheet in water, then put on body. In one night, ten to thirteen sheets, like that. Then Dr. Herbert Benson of Harvard became interested in tumo. They came to Dharamsala and did some tests on tumo experts living in the mountains. They were very impressed by Tenzin's ability to generate body heat. So, with my permission, they invited him to do some tests at Harvard."

Karma Gelek, a young monk who spoke English well, accompanied Tenzin to the United States. He told me that their 1985 trip was a difficult one. Tenzin arrived in Boston with a severe case of jet lag. He was exhausted and wanted to postpone the tumo experiments until he acclimatized. But Dr. Benson's lab ran on a very tight schedule; it was impossible to delay. The experiments started the next day.

Tenzin was subjected to an exhaustive battery of tests in a lab where the temperature was kept at meat-cooler levels. The experimenters wore down vests under their white lab coats. Tenzin was made to take off his upper robes, and was left wearing only a thin cotton vest. The tests took forever. According to Gelek, Tenzin was frozen to the core during the session.

When Tenzin finally entered into a deep state of meditation, his oxygen intake dropped spectacularly; with a corresponding reduction in metabolism, he needed to take only five or six breaths a minute, compared to the normal thirteen or fourteen. By the time tumo was generated, his body temperature had risen by a good ten degrees. Dr. Benson wrote later in his study of tumo practitioners (*MindScience: An East-*

West Dialogue, the Dalai Lama et al., Wisdom Publications, 1991): "What we are finding through these experiments is that meditative processes lead to rather striking physiological changes in the body. These changes have direct health implications . . . any disorder is caused or made worse by stress."

I was intrigued by Lobsang Tenzin's story. I wondered how a freedom fighter, a man used to taking lives, could develop such powerful spiritual prowess relatively late in life. Most Tibetan monks, for example, begin their training in the monastery when they are six or seven.

Karma Gelek told me that Tenzin believed his spiritual practice began and then dramatically improved during his time in Chinese prison. It was during this difficult period that he came to two insights. First, he realized his suffering in prison was karmically linked, a direct result of his own atrocities against the Chinese. Second, he intuited that if he allowed himself to be consumed with hatred for the Chinese, if his focus remained on revenge, he would drive himself insane.

Despite his lack of control over what the Chinese could do to him physically, Tenzin finally understood that the Chinese could not damage his mental health unilaterally. The only way his psychological well-being could suffer was through his own attitude, his own reaction to his dire straits. He knew that if he could develop a neutral—or, better yet, a positive—feeling toward his captors, he would be able to sleep at night. And no matter how badly the Chinese tortured him, his mind would always be a safe haven for him to retreat to.

According to Gelek, Tenzin sublimated his hatred for the Chinese. He simply forgave them. Over time, he even developed genuine compassion for them. That proved to be the key. That was how he survived his harsh imprisonment with very little damage to his mental state. While in prison, he belatedly came to believe in the healing power of forgiveness. Gelek thinks that this was what allowed Tenzin to make the quantum leap in his spiritual practice. His prowess in tumo increased dramatically as well.

So TO BE ABLE to forgive your enemies can make a difference to one's spiritual progress?" I asked the Dalai Lama.

"Yes, yes, there is no doubt," he replied. "It's crucial. It's one of most important thing. It can change one's life. To reduce hatred and other destructive emotions, you must develop their opposites—compassion and kindness. If you have strong compassion, strong respect for others, then forgiveness much easier. Mainly for this reason: I do not want to harm another. Forgiveness allows you to be in touch with these positive emotions. This will help with spiritual development."

"Is there a special meditation technique that you use?" I asked.

"I use meditation technique called giving and taking," the

Dalai Lama explained. "I make visualization: send my positive emotions like happiness, affection to others. Then another visualization. I visualize receiving their sufferings, their negative emotions. I do this every day. I pay special attention to the Chinese—especially those doing terrible things to the Tibetans. So, as I meditate, I breathe in all their poisons—hatred, fear, cruelty. Then I breathe out. And I let all the good things come out, things like compassion, forgiveness. I take inside my body all these bad things. Then I replace poisons with fresh air. Giving and taking. I take care not to blame— I don't blame the Chinese, and I don't blame myself. This meditation very effective, useful to reduce hatred, useful to cultivate forgiveness."

5.

A Most Altruistic Person

The Nobel Centennial festivities in Oslo were in full swing. I was sitting in the mezzanine lounge of the venerable Holmenkollen Hotel, waiting to have a drink with Lodi Gyari Rinpoche, the special envoy of His Holiness the Dalai Lama. The lounge was busy. I could see Holocaust writer and Nobel Peace laureate Elie Wiesel deep in conversation with a companion, totally oblivious to the hubbub around him. Another laureate, José Ramos-Hortas of East Timor, was at an adjacent table; he was being interviewed by a couple of journalists.

From my table I had a good view of the hotel lobby below. State-of-the-art metal detectors were stationed at the entrance. Half a dozen Norwegian police, impeccable in their snug-fitting uniforms, checked everyone who entered. During these celebrations, Oslo was deploying wartime-like security measures. Earlier, on my way into the Holmenkollen, I had spotted a few police sharpshooters, conspicuous in their battle fatigues, lurking at strategic spots on the rooftop. A pair of F-16 jet fighters was on permanent high alert. In the next few days, they would enforce a temporary no-fly zone over Oslo.

Lodi Gyari arrived fifteen minutes late and slightly harried. He had just come from a meeting between the Dalai Lama and Richard Holbrooke in the Tibetan monk's hotel suite. Holbrooke, the American diplomat who had brokered the Balkan peace treaty in 1995, was in town for the celebrations. As usual, Lodi was dressed in an elegantly tailored suit, perhaps Savile Row. Round of face and heavyset, he had the polished, unfailingly polite look of an immensely successful Asian businessman.

Lodi Gyari, together with Tenzin Geyche Tethong, is one of the Dalai Lama's closest advisers. After his boss, Lodi Gyari is arguably the most effective advocate for Tibet in the West. I wanted to glean some insights about the Tibetan leader from the one man who has been his confidant for four decades.

"What's it like to work for the Dalai Lama?" I asked him.

"Everyone knows that His Holiness is very compassionate," Gyari replied. "But he's also a very strong-willed person; this is something people working close to him know. This draws people like me to him."

"His strength," I said.

"Yes, there is no doubt his compassion is all-encompassing.

But to be frank, he is not an easy boss. And the yardstick with which he measures you is phenomenal. I'm very conscious that I work for someone who has high ideals. This is useful because it restrains me. I won't cross certain limits in my personal conduct.

"Let me tell you something that happened during the Tiananmen Square incident," Lodi Gyari said. "I was his foreign minister when the tragedy occurred. At that time, despite several ups and downs, we were on the verge of starting a dialogue with the Chinese. Yang Minfu was the head of the United Front Works department, and somehow we had managed to reestablish contact. There was agreement in principle for a preliminary meeting in Hong Kong, which would set the actual venue and the date of negotiations."

I knew that there is nothing more crucial for the Dalai Lama and the other exiled Tibetans than to coax the Chinese to the negotiating table. Everything they have worked for in the past four decades is geared toward this objective. The consensus among many thoughtful Tibetans is that a genuine rapprochement with the Chinese is the only way to save the Tibetan way of life and stop Tibet from being swamped by a tidal wave of Chinese migrants. But despite the prodigious moral authority of the Dalai Lama, the Chinese have rarely shown signs that they're willing to talk.

Gyari continued. "I was busy preparing for that, and then Tiananmen Square happened. I remember it well. I was at home in Dharamsala. One of His Holiness' drivers came with a vehicle to fetch me; I was wanted immediately in the palace.

I quickly put on my Tibetan dress; the driver had instructions to bring me to His Holiness' residence instead of the office. When I arrived, Tenzin Geyche was already waiting for me. The two of us went straight to the Dalai Lama's room.

"For the first time ever, I saw that His Holiness was very, very agitated. He was like Napoleon. He didn't turn around to face us when we walked in; he had his hands clasped behind his back. He was deep in thought. He dispensed with the usual greetings and immediately asked us: 'Did you see? Did you see?'

"Of course we had seen. There was nothing else on TV; we knew what he was referring to. So we said yes. He said, 'You two get to work on a statement I want to issue: the strongest condemnation of the Chinese government and their policy of brutalizing their own people, my unconditional support for the youngsters on the Square.'

"My selfish Tibetan mind immediately said: 'Oh, my God, this is going to ruin any opportunities for negotiations, something we have worked hard on for decades.' His Holiness turned, read my body language right away, and said curtly: 'What is it?' I said, 'Your Holiness, of course you realize this will derail our efforts at negotiations, maybe for a very long time.' I felt that he had registered my views, and for one brief moment I thought he would modify his position. But then he turned around. I felt intense energy, like that of a tiger. He said, 'Yes, it's true, you have a point. But if I do not speak out now, I have no moral right to ever speak out for freedom and democracy. Those young people are asking for nothing more, nothing less than what I have been asking for. And if I can't speak for them' "—Lodi hesitated, searching his memory for the right words—" 'I'll be ashamed to ever talk about freedom and democracy.' "

Lodi grew silent. Out of habit, I tried to keep my face impassive. But it was difficult. I was deeply moved by the Dalai Lama's response. He had squarely placed the welfare of the Chinese students ahead of the hopes of his countrymen. I looked away. The hum of conversation in the crowded lounge continued, unabated.

"I felt a tremendous respect for His Holiness," Gyari went on. "I also felt very small, very selfish. Of course, in retrospect, I was right in my assessment that His Holiness' stance would kill the negotiations. Deng Xiaopeng never forgave him. He took it very personally, as we learned later on. But it is things like this that make me feel honored to serve His Holiness, because he is genuine. He believes in what he preaches, and he acts according to that."

*L*ODI GYARI and I had been chatting in the mezzanine lounge of the Holmenkollen Hotel for more than an hour. Gyari was a wonderful raconteur, and I was hanging on his every word. There was some commotion in the lobby downstairs. We looked over the railing to see that Archbishop Desmond Tutu had just entered the hotel. Resplendent in his formal scarlet robes, the South African was grinning from ear to ear and radiating megawatt goodwill.

As we sat back in our chairs, Gyari picked up his story again. "His Holiness' first-ever visit to Europe was in 1973," he said. "I was very young, very radical in those days. Halfway into our six-week tour, we were in Switzerland. His Holiness was staying at a private home near Zurich. I was beginning to feel frustrated because so far he had said very little about Tibet in public."

"He was talking about religion instead?" I asked.

"He was talking about the things he talks about all the time—universal responsibility, compassion, the good heart. But lots of people also wanted to know about Tibet. I felt he was not doing enough for the Tibetan people. I remember well the house he was staying in, a huge chalet, full of beautiful stained-glass windows. One early morning, I walked into his room. He knew immediately that I was agitated, that I had something on my mind."

"He could read you very well," I said.

"Yes. He said to me: 'What is it?' I said, 'Your Holiness, I think you should speak more about Tibet. This is a tremendous opportunity; we need to tell the world more about the suffering of our people.' He said: 'It's true, yes, I understand. In fact, I have also thought I should talk more about Tibet. But you know, many of these people have so many problems on their minds. They come to me with some kind of false hope that I'll be able to lift their burden, which I can't. I feel that I have no right to send them out with an extra burden: a burden of my own.' Tears came into my eyes when I heard that."

Lodi Gyari paused and looked away. I could tell he was moved by that memory. Finally it was time for him to leave. As we stood up, his eyes held mine. "Victor, I'm sure of one thing. His Holiness is the most altruistic person I know."

Gyari gave me a bear hug, then walked out of the hotel to a waiting car. He would miss most of the historic Nobel Centennial celebrations in Oslo. As always, he had a plane to catch.

6.

No Rubber Duckies

⁂ There was a frisson of excitement in the Dalai Lama's private chapel in Dharamsala, transformed for five days into a conference room for the Tenth Mind and Life Conference. All eyes were on Steven Chu, the American Nobel laureate in physics. He sat on the presenter's seat to the right of the Dalai Lama, a tall brass vase overflowing with fresh-cut flowers behind him. Chu was gearing up to explain the subtle relationship between mathematics and quantum mechanics to the Dalai Lama and the assembled guests.

"What is math?" he began by asking the Tibetan leader. I was unprepared for the question; I could see the Dalai Lama was slightly taken aback too. When he didn't reply, Chu continued, "Well, math strikes fear into most people."

The room erupted into laughter. With two short sentences, Chu had managed to put everyone at ease. Eric Lander, the Boston geneticist sitting to the right of Chu, wrapped his beefy arms around his chest. The Dalai Lama, seated in his customary lotus position in a comfortable armchair, smiled as he swayed lightly from side to side.

Chu tapped a key on his laptop computer on the low table before him. A slide showing three rows of yellow toy ducks flashed onto the screen erected at one end of the room: one duck in the first row, two in the middle, and three at the bottom. "This is a technical thing. It's called a rubber ducky. We put it in a bathtub," Chu said, pointing a red laser beam at the lone duck on top. "So this is one ducky, two duckies, three duckies. We can add duckies . . ."

There was pandemonium in the small conference hall. Lander clapped his hand on his thigh and roared. Chu choked in mid-sentence, his prominent Adam's apple jiggling up and down. For a minute or two, he lost control as a tidal wave of mirth took over his trim frame.

The swaying Dalai Lama still had a smile on his face. But there was a sphinx-like quality to it. He seemed a touch removed, not quite his usual self. Somehow I had expected him to laugh the loudest.

Thupten Jinpa, the Dalai Lama's translator, leaned in close and spoke to him in Tibetan.

A thought crossed my mind: perhaps the Dalai Lama was culturally challenged. He had probably never played with rubber duckies in his bathtub. Rubber duckies were most likely unheard of in Tibet. He simply couldn't understand what the fuss was all about.

"We can check this experimentally," the geneticist yelled, still gripped by a paroxysm of laughter.

"Actually, it has been checked experimentally many, many times," Steve Chu said, pulling himself together with difficulty. "In a certain sense, that is reality. So we know how to add duckies. Now, if you have two duckies and take *away* one, you get one ducky. But what if you have one ducky: is it possible to take away two?" He looked over at the Dalai Lama, shrugged, and spread his arms. "What is happening here?" Chu asked. "Well, all of a sudden, something new is going on. The process of subtraction led mathematicians to invent negative numbers. Then we made up rules—the rules for addition and subtraction, for example. This led to complex numbers . . . numbers that include the square root of minus one in their makeup. And it is complex numbers that allow us to describe quantum mechanics."

The Private Office of the Dalai Lama had given me permission to attend the Dharamsala conference. About fifty of us, scientists, invited guests, and a small group of Tibetan monks, were crowded into the small hall inside the Dalai Lama's residential compound. The topic was "The Nature of Matter, The Nature of Life," and the presenters included world-renowned specialists in complexity, genomic research, evolutionary biology, Buddhist philosophy, and, of course, physics. There had been regular encounters between the Dalai Lama and a diverse group of Western neurologists, physicists, and philosophers since 1987. Past dialogues have triggered several scientific research projects and spawned numerous publications.

I loved the easy camaraderie of the scientists, and I appreciated Steve Chu's sense of humor. The bespectacled physicist had been the cowinner of the Nobel Prize in 1997. He had found a way to use laser light to cool gases, slowing atoms down from their usual speed of 4,000 kilometers an hour at room temperature to two centimeters in the same time period. He then kept them floating in a kind of atom trap, with the laser light functioning as what he had dubbed "optical molasses."

Chu was obviously excited to be in Dharamsala. He relished the idea of explaining matter and life to the Dalai Lama from a physicist's perspective. Shortly before launching into his theory of rubber duckies, he had reminded the Tibetan of their first meeting.

"Your Holiness," Chu said, "perhaps you remember . . . we met six years ago at Stanford. We had a discussion with several people, from morning until lunch. It was a very important event in my life." The last sentence was spoken quietly, and Chu blinked several times. Then, regaining his composure, he continued in his usual laid-back style: "Since coming here, I've learned a great deal. Maybe a little from my Western colleagues, but mostly from you, and from the Tibetan monks. I hope, in the days to come, I can continue to learn more."

That kind of learning exchange was the purpose of the Mind and Life conferences, as the Dalai Lama had envisaged them. He hoped scientists could open up new directions of exploration by learning to look at reality from a Buddhist perspective. And he thought Buddhists could take home useful insights about modern science.

"My interest and close contact with scientists—now more than fifteen years," the Dalai Lama had told me. "It seems to me more and more scientists begin to show genuine interest in dialogue with Buddhists. I feel something useful, not only satisfying my own interest. The dialogue between scientists and Buddhists can help expand human knowledge. We have already introduced scientific study to some selected Tibetan monks for the last two, three years. I feel personally we started something right, something of benefit to the larger community."

But the Dalai Lama had another motive for convening these meetings between Buddhists and scientists, one he saw as being of paramount importance.

"Everybody wants a happy life—more calm, more peaceful, more satisfactory life," he continued, explaining his involvement with scientists to me. "For this, the development of the inner world—emotions, these things—is important. I'm not referring to religious faith. I'm not talking about heaven, liberation, or next life. Our concern is happier individuals, happier communities. We want to promote human values: a sense of caring, sense of sharing. The result: we become more open and our perspectives become wider. When we come across problems, their disturbances on our inner peace are less severe.

"Ancient Indian thought contributes knowledge and technique to take care of inner life. Science of course also has tremendous responsibility. But I feel developing inner values more important. Look at the event in New York on September eleventh. It clearly shows how modern technology, combined with human intelligence and guided by negative emotions such as hatred, can create disaster—something very immense. Really bring suffering to lots of people. To utilize technology more constructively, inner peace is the most important factor. That's the main reason to have closer relation between modern science and ancient human thought. Side by side, some way to make contribution to a better world."

I had been intrigued when Steven Chu recounted his first meeting with the Dalai Lama. It obviously was a significant event for him. When the physicist's presentation was over, I asked Chu whether he would like to meet with the Dalai Lama and me privately. He told me that the thought of an audience hadn't crossed his mind. He had come to Dharamsala for one reason only: he wanted to know what Buddhism has to say about cutting-edge physics. But now that I'd broached the idea, Chu was excited. Yes, he'd be honored to meet with the Tibetan leader.

ON THE LAST DAY of the conference, Steve Chu, his wife, Jean, and I squeezed onto a couch in the audience room, across from the Dalai Lama. The Chinese American was dressed simply in a light blue shirt and beige slacks. He wore a pair of scruffy tennis shoes—he was known as an avid tennis player at Stanford. Tenzin Geyche, looking scholarly and distinguished in gray Tibetan robes, sat apart from us.

"Yesterday, when you spoke at the conference, you showed Asian tradition," the Dalai Lama said to Chu right away. "Humbleness. You expressed limitation of your knowledge. But when your explanation came, full authority."

"When we scientists explain, we always remind ourselves: this we know, this we don't know," Chu replied.

"That's right. I notice genuine scientists . . . they're unbiased observers. Not much mental projection; always trying to know reality," the Dalai Lama said.

"We try," Chu said.

"So. Nobel laureate. Chinese origin. And this, my old friend," the Dalai Lama pointed a finger at me, "also supposedly Chinese origin. Almost like a semi-Chinese now." His famous baritone laugh filled the audience room. He made fun of my Western ways at every turn.

"Usually, when I come here to see His Holiness, I'm the only Chinese among all these Tibetans. This time I get some support," I said, patting the Chinese American on the knee. "But there is a difference: here's one smart Chinese and one rather dumb one. I understood perfectly the part about the rubber duckies. But the rest was all physics to me."

Chu smiled, shaking his head.

The Dalai Lama scooted forward in his chair, focusing his attention on the scientist.

"Day before yesterday, one geneticist talked to us about his research center in Boston," the Dalai Lama said. "Then he told us there are branches in Europe, even one in Peking. So I felt that scientists really represent humanity. Nothing to do with race, nation, or ideology. They just carry on research, irrespective of these other things."

"That's right, for most scientists, anyway," Chu said.

"We need this spirit among the politicians, among world leaders," the Dalai Lama continued. "Sometimes they focus too much on their own ideologies, their own nations. Then unnecessary problems come. That's unfortunate. Take the Chinese and the Tibetans. For two thousand years, we had close relations. Sometimes fighting, killing each other. Sometimes close friends. Nowadays, things are difficult."

The Dalai Lama sighed audibly and continued: "My main concern not Tibetan race or nation alone. My main concern Tibetan tradition: a combination of Buddhism, logic, and philosophy. It not only an ancient culture, it is also quite sophisticated and relevant in today's world—how to know more about our emotions, how to transform our emotions. I feel that the preservation of Tibetan spirituality not only of interest to six million Tibetans; it's for a larger community. Particularly for our Chinese brothers and sisters. They have lost so much of their rich heritage. Tibetan Buddhist tradition can make a contribution; its preservation is of mutual benefit."

"Professor Chu," I interjected, "you have strong contacts with the academic community in China. What's your sense of Chinese thinking on Tibet?"

"Most people get their information about Tibet from government-controlled sources," Chu replied. "They say, well, we have to be careful: the Dalai Lama is very cunning. Not the professors, but certainly the young people. But things are changing. It's becoming much harder for the government to control the press, especially the Internet. It has tried; it actually tried to get rid of Google. For a few weeks the authorities managed to direct all searches to government search engines. But it failed in the end. Too many people knew how to get around it."

"Also, more and more Chinese are traveling to Tibet," the Dalai Lama added. "Previously pure tourists. Nowadays, many of them come to Tibet as pilgrims. Recently, I heard that the Tibetan monks in Lhasa make around six thousand yuans a year. Equivalent . . ."

"About eight hundred dollars U.S.," I offered.

"No, no, no . . . I meant to say . . ." The Dalai Lama was clearly getting frustrated that he had trouble getting his point across. He turned to Tenzin Geyche and spoke to him in Tibetan.

"His Holiness says the offering made to the monks almost equal . . ." Geyche began.

"No, no, no," the Dalai Lama interrupted. He had finally found the words to frame his thoughts properly. "The money monks receive a year from the Chinese tourists is almost same as salary of the party cadres working for the government. Their income not come from Tibetans, therefore, but mainly from Chinese pilgrims. So, although the Tibetans' situation is difficult, a lot of repression, they already are exploiting money from the Chinese." He laughed uproariously.

Jean Chu seemed mesmerized by the Dalai Lama's unrestrained display of merriment. Tenzin Geyche, normally a model of restraint, had a big grin on his face.

"These are positive signs," the Dalai Lama went on. "Some Tibetan lamas now give teachings to many Chinese. One lama in east Tibet has ordained six hundred Chinese Buddhists. These are clear indications that many Chinese show genuine interest in Tibetan culture. Still, we need to make friends with more Chinese. The best people to do that are American Chinese, Canadian Chinese."

Chu looked thoughtful. "I go to China maybe once a year now, and I see more and more people willing to discuss real issues," he said. "In a private group like this, they actually talk about what the government is doing. I can probably get into a discussion about Tibet . . ." He hesitated, then pressed on. "And I'd ask why we haven't had this discussion. But it's not only the Tibetan culture. It's Falun Gong, anything spiritual."

"That's right, that's right," the Dalai Lama agreed.

Nobody spoke for a while. There was a companionable silence in the room. Then I remembered that there was something else I wanted to ask Steven Chu.

"Yesterday in your presentation, you said that when you first met His Holiness in Stanford, it was a very important moment in your life. Why?"

Chu directed his reply to the Dalai Lama. "It was my first exposure to you. Before the meeting, I had read your biography. I really didn't know what to expect. As a scientist, I was a little skeptical. Well, we'll see, I thought. And then . . . the way you handled yourself. You were smiling right away. It struck me that it was true, some of the things I'd heard about you. I saw you as a very warm person, a very gentle person, someone who really liked other people, even those you don't know. I immediately felt that at the meeting. The fact that you can project something like that in so short a time had a profound impact on me."

Chu paused. "I have an undergraduate working in my lab," he went on. "Very smart, grew up in Hong Kong. I told him, 'I'm going to visit the Dalai Lama.' He got a little excited, and he said the Dalai Lama was probably a sneaky politician."

Everyone in the room laughed.

"I told him, 'I meet politicians; they act very differently,' " Chu continued. "The student said, 'But he's the head of state.' 'Yes,' I replied, 'he's the head of state, but I don't think he's a politician.' "

The Dalai Lama shifted position until he was sitting on the edge of his chair. Hunched forward, with his forearms resting comfortably on his knees, he stared into space as he launched into an anecdote.

"Many years ago," he said, "I met this Chinese. He studied Chinese Buddhism, Confucius. He worked in America. His friends, Chinese businessmen in New York, told him, 'The Dalai Lama is not a religious person; he's mainly a politician. Other Tibetan lamas, there are some true spiritual masters there. But the Dalai Lama is not one of them.' So he was reluctant to come to my teachings. But out of curiosity, he came. Then he noticed: Dalai Lama quite honest, quite compassionate. He found out more about me, and he examined closely my behavior. Eventually, he became my close spiritual friend. He called me his teacher; in fact, he was ordained by me. So not only the Communists but also the general public has this false idea. Since I'm responsible for Tibet, the media has created the impression that the Dalai Lama is not a simple Buddhist monk, he is mainly a politician."

He paused for effect. Then he said, "Hopefully, a tough politician."

After the laughter had subsided, the Dalai Lama turned to Jean Chu, who had been sitting quietly. "You have something to say?"

"We visited the Tibetan children's village last night," she said, "and the thing that impressed me was how you have managed to maintain your culture here in Dharamsala. You have moved from your homeland but still managed to maintain your identity. I think that's a tremendous example for other people."

The Dalai Lama started to reply, changed his mind, and spoke to Tenzin Geyche in Tibetan.

"Your comment is a great encouragement," Geyche translated.

"Yes," the Dalai Lama said. "Right from the beginning, forty-three years ago, our main concern is the preservation of Tibetan culture—establishing schools, children's village, these things. And we created separate Tibetan colonies in South India. Same principle: to keep our culture. Now, I'm proud to say, pure Tibetan tradition, pure Buddhist knowledge, is available outside of Tibet."

"The wonderful thing we've learned about Buddhism here is that it is very open," Jean added. "It has the ability to accept a different kind of thinking, to incorporate that thinking into your society so that it can be enriched."

"Thank you," the Dalai Lama said. "That's why every young Tibetan now in India, their only aim is: go to America."

He had another good belly laugh. Then it was time to walk up the hill back to the conference.

7.

Diamonds on the Net

The Dalai Lama got out of the white armor-plated Ambassador and shuffled toward a makeshift podium erected next to the imposing Sarnath stupa. A few hundred pilgrims and monks had gathered, waiting for him to deliver a teaching. It was January, and the Tibetan leader was about to embark on a rare pilgrimage to India's most sacred Buddhist sites. Sarnath was the first stop. Two dozen high lamas in their trademark maroon robes, holding thick sticks of incense in their hands, lined the path to welcome him.

I was struck by the Dalai Lama's terrible posture—he was bent nearly double as he walked toward them. Like many Tibetan monks, he had rounded shoulders that scooted forward to give the appearance of a hunch—a subconscious body language intimating humility, which, over time, ossified into a permanent condition. The Dalai Lama greeted the lamas, the most illustrious in the Tibetan Buddhist pantheon, with warmth and easy camaraderie. These elderly spiritual masters competed relentlessly to see who could bow the lowest.

As he approached his marigold-encrusted throne on the podium, the Tibetan leader paused and stared at the ten-story-high monument, an unusual-looking structure that vaguely resembled a gargantuan Soviet two-stage rocket—except that its top was flat rather than streamlined. Built two centuries ago, and buffeted by monsoon rain every summer, it was a minor miracle that the structure still stood. It was clad completely in bamboo scaffolding in preparation for a major renovation. Along the lower rungs, pilgrims had tied numerous white offering scarves.

The stupa marks the site where the Buddha gave his first sermon, immediately after he attained enlightenment under the bodhi tree in Bodhgaya. For many, Sarnath is synonymous with the birthplace of Buddhism. For 1,500 years after the death of the Buddha, the religion flourished in India until the Muslim invasion. However, over the past thirty years, Sarnath has once again become a center of Buddhist thought. A dozen new temples and monasteries, representing every branch of Buddhism, have been built, and worshippers flock here during pilgrimage season.

The Dalai Lama had told me that Sarnath is one place in India that elicited great emotional responses from him. He was here on pilgrimage very soon after his escape from Tibet in 1959. A crowd of 2,000 destitute Tibetans, who crossed the

Himalayas into exile weeks earlier, waited for him in front of the great stupa. They were in bad shape: most had lost relatives on the trek; some were terribly frostbitten. With only the clothes on their back and a few pieces of hastily salvaged heirloom, they arrived on the steamy plains of Sarnath and set up makeshift stalls to eke out a living.

When the then twenty-four-year-old Dalai Lama saw the crowd, he broke down and wept openly. Everything he had experienced during those tumultuous few months—the ever-increasing Chinese repression in Lhasa, the harrowing escape over the Himalayas, the final realization that he had become a refugee—all crystallized at that moment. The conflicting emotions he had bottled up broke through. And he wept as he had never wept before.

M Y FIRST-EVER MEETING with the Dalai Lama took place in March 1972. I still remember how apprehensive I was on that occasion. I didn't know much about Sino-Tibetan relations then, but I knew one thing: the Chinese had killed a great many Tibetans in the occupation of their country. I had been anxious about the Tibetan leader's reaction toward me. After all, I had been the first Chinese to sit across from him since his exile a decade earlier.

"As you may remember," I said to the Dalai Lama in a recent interview in Dharamsala, "in my first audience with you back in 1972, the question uppermost in my mind was whether you hated the Chinese. You told me you don't hate them; you told me you have truly forgiven them. Your Holiness, this was just thirteen years after you'd lost your country. I was very surprised at your magnanimity."

"That's Buddhist training," the Dalai Lama replied. "Not something unique in my case. Quite a number of Tibetan practitioners have similar sort of attitude. Forgiveness and compassion are important parts of practice."

"How do you feel about the Chinese these days?"

"I think you notice my feelings toward the Chinese, in teachings here and also in Taiwan," the Dalai Lama replied. "Whether religious persons, ordinary people, Taiwanese officials, even Taiwanese bodyguards, I'm very friendly. This friendly response, perhaps because I spoke broken Chinese since my childhood in northeastern Tibet. So that's fact. If Chinese showing genuine friendship, then my response very automatic—because of this factor. But anyway, wherever I go, whenever I met someone, whether black African or Indian or Chinese or European, not much difference, I think."

I didn't say so, but I don't think that was entirely correct. I think the Dalai Lama has always gone out of his way to connect with the Chinese, especially those from the mainland. He invests a great deal of himself in these encounters, and quite often they are fraught with emotion for him. I remembered his meeting in Washington, D.C., with Wang Lixiong, the well-known Chinese author. Wang was the first Chinese to write authoritatively and impartially about the current situation in Tibet.

Their get-together was unusual. Instead of receiving

Wang in his hotel suite as was his custom, the Dalai Lama waited for the Chinese writer near the elevator, alongside his bodyguards and his senior aides. This was a gesture of respect he does not extend to too many people—at least, I've seldom seen it. The Dalai Lama greeted Wang warmly in Chinese: *"Ni hao."* Then he led him by the hand back to his suite. They sat down on couches next to the black Steinway baby grand, facing each other in silence: the maroon-robed monk and the writer in a dark blue Chinese jacket. Suddenly the Dalai Lama reached out and pulled Wang toward him. He firmly touched his forehead to Wang's. Ten, twenty seconds passed. As they stepped apart, Wang could see that the Tibetan's eyes were moist. Wang would later write, in a book recounting their conversations: "Maybe he took me to be the representative of the Chinese who for generations lived in the land near the Tibetans. Though he had met a few Chinese in the past, they were mostly émigrés who no longer had their roots in China."

"Now, the question why my warm feelings toward the Chinese," the Dalai Lama continued with his train of thought. "My whole sort of feelings, thinking, from viewpoint of interdependence. For example, while I was in Taiwan, I met DDP [Democratic Progressive Party, the ruling party of Taiwan] leaders. I told them, as far as Tibet is concerned, I'm not seeking independence. And I told them Taiwan should also think carefully about her ties with China. Taiwan needs special, unique close relation with China, for economy reasons, as well as in defense, things like that. So whole globe heavily interdependent. Tibet economically, environmentally, heavily dependent on Chinese. Chinese more prosperous, benefit Tibetans—if we remain in China. If we separate, in long run, Tibetans may face more difficulty.

"My middle-way approach: not separate from China—economically bound to the PRC [People's Republic of China]. Meanwhile, full autonomy, self-government. Culture, education, environment, spirituality: these things we Tibetans can manage better. I'm quite sure that our Tibetan traditions, Tibetan spirituality, can help millions of Chinese. Already some Chinese artists, some Chinese thinkers are showing interest in Tibet, in Tibetan Buddhism. So China and Tibet. Not separate. Help each other, interdependent."

Like so many of the issues he cares deeply about, his Sino-Tibetan policies are driven by his Buddhist view of the interdependence of all things—insights that he had internalized, like a cloth soaked in oil, when he was in his late twenties. To him, the reality of life is like the celebrated Indra's Net of ancient mythology. The universe is looked upon as an enormous web woven of innumerable strands of thread. A diamond is affixed to each juncture. Any one diamond, with its countless facets, perfectly reflects all other diamonds—like an infinite array of halls of mirrors—and each has an ineffable relationship with all others. Disturbances in one area of the net galvanize a ripple effect that impacts, however subtly, on other parts. It is like the Butterfly Effect. The flapping of a butterfly's wings in Beijing could cause minuscule atmospheric changes, which over time could affect weather patterns in Vancouver.

On a human level, my daughters will not sleep safely in their beds if kids in Kabul or Baghdad are not safe in theirs. For the Dalai Lama, the reality of life is an integrated whole: all things are interrelated, and nothing exists independently. There is a well-known Tibetan saying: all beings have at some time been our mothers, just as we have at some time been theirs. It encourages us to work hard at self-restraint and to cultivate consideration for the welfare of others. I grasped the idea intuitively, but I still find myself struggling for a deeper understanding.

The Dalai Lama continued: "In my own case, in Tibet, all this destruction, death, all happened. Painful experiences. But revenge . . . this creates more unhappiness. So, think wider perspective: revenge no good, so forgive. Forgiveness does not mean you just forget about the past. No, you remember the past. Should be aware that these past sufferings happened because of narrow-mindedness on both sides. So now, time passed. We feel more wise, more developed. I think that's the only way."

"How do you foster forgiveness?" I asked.

"First, according to my own experience, I think of others, including my so-called enemies. These people also human beings. They also have the same right to achieve happiness and avoid suffering. Freshness, smiles, everybody likes. Crime, bloodshed, nobody likes. Then second. My future related with them; my interest related with their interest. For example: my country, my people, very much related with the Chinese. Our future very much depends on them. Taking care of them is ultimately taking care of ourselves."

"But how do the Chinese affect you personally?" I asked the Dalai Lama. "Perhaps there were personal tragedies that touched you directly because of the Chinese invasion?"

"Personally, not much. But when I heard, for example, from one Tibetan who was put in Chinese prison. He still alive, now living in Nepal. He told me in his prison, there was one Tibetan boy." The Dalai Lama had shifted position in his deep, comfortable armchair and was now perching on the edge, his hands gripping the armrests.

"The boy was at that time sixteen years old; according to Chinese constitution, not yet reached age of punishment. But he was in prison and about to be executed because his father fought the Chinese. One day Chinese soldiers came with guns. One officer looked around, found an iron rod, picked it up, and beat that boy whose father had killed some of the officer's soldiers. In revenge, to satisfy himself, the officer beat the young boy, who was going to die in any case, with that iron rod. When I heard that . . ." The Dalai Lama raised his hands to his eyes. "Tears came into my eyes."

I was affected by the tragic story, the terrible things that grown men could do to the young and innocent. But my overriding emotion at that moment was shame. I was disgusted, and I felt guilty—by association. Like some other Chinese I know, I have the habit of identifying with the behavior of ethnic Chinese, no matter where they live. When I read in Vancouver that a Chinese restaurant in Shanghai served dogs to their customers, I cringed involuntarily.

"How does this story of the Tibetan boy affect your view of the Chinese? How does the concept of interdependence come into this?" I asked after a pause.

"First I was angry, then I felt sorry for the officer," the Dalai Lama replied. "The officer's action depends on his motivation; his motivation depends on propaganda. Because of propaganda, the counterrevolutionary father is seen as evil. Elimination of evil is something positive. That kind of faith—wrong faith. You can't blame that person. Under circumstances like that, even I myself may act like that. So, thinking along this line, instead of anger, forgiveness and compassion came. Interdependence gives you whole picture: this happens because of that, and that happens because of this. Clear?"

The Dalai Lama has this uncanny ability to put himself in the other person's shoes. Especially if that person is his enemy. As he has told me before, he considers his enemies to be his most valuable teachers. He loves and cherishes his friends. But he believes it is our enemies who can truly provide us with the challenge we need to cultivate qualities like forgiveness and compassion. Forgiveness and compassion, in turn, are essential ingredients for peace of mind.

"The essence of Buddhism: one side compassion, one side viewpoint of interdependence," the Dalai Lama continued. "And I always tell people, it's very important to make distinction: actor and act. We have to oppose bad action. But that does not mean we against that person, actor. Once action stopped, different action come, then that person could be friend. That's why today Chinese is enemy; the next day, there's always the possibility to become friend. And that's why I have no problems forgiving the Chinese for what they've done to my country and people."

The Dalai Lama relaxed, slumping against the back of his armchair. Then he said, unprompted: "But if I was on the spot and meet the Chinese soldier, the officer who beat that boy . . . If I was there, and I have gun, then I don't know." He raised his right hand from its resting position on his abdomen, fingers holding an imaginary gun. A mischievous smile played across his lips.

"Such moment, I may shoot the Chinese," the Dalai Lama said, shrugging his shoulders. He lifted his arms and spread them wide. Then he started to chuckle.

I didn't share in the laughter. It was a stretch for me to imagine the scenario. I asked the Dalai Lama: "Even with your Buddhist training?"

"Possible. Under such tense circumstances, possible. Sometimes, thinking comes later. Action comes first."

8.

A Rifle in the Bedroom

🖋 Among the ancient ruins of the University of Nalanda, the afternoon sun was warm and pleasant. The Dalai Lama and an entourage of about a hundred monks sat and recited prayers in the grassy area directly across from the remains of a ninety-foot-high stupa. They came here after spending time in Sarnath, on a rare pilgrimage to pay homage to the pre-eminent Indian Buddhists who had studied and taught at Nalanda. The Tibetan leader had not been here for more than two decades.

A white dog appeared out of nowhere and ambled up to the assembled monks. He picked a spot close to them and sat down, his head cocked quizzically toward the Dalai Lama. After he'd sat there for a while, seemingly tuning in to the deep baritone chants, he lay down and went to sleep.

I walked to the red-brick stupa, a striking thousand-year-old ruin that resembled a gigantic, stand-alone stairway. Clambering over half-walls, I soon reached a small roofless chapel. In a niche on one wall was a bas-relief of a deity. The delicately carved image, sweet and elegant, was in pristine condition. The deity's hip and shoulders were articulated in opposing directions to suggest movement. The face was heart-shaped, a gentle smile played on the lips. There was a palpable sense of inner peace about the image. I stood there, transfixed, as I listened to the soothing Tibetan prayers.

The Dalai Lama is well aware of the huge debt Tibetan Buddhism owed the Indian Buddhist masters who lived and taught at Nalanda from the second through the ninth centuries C.E.—the Golden Age of Indic thought. Nalanda was the largest and the most renowned university in ancient India. The Buddhist kings of Gupta and Pala were devoted patrons. For a thousand years Nalanda, the Harvard of its day, attracted the best and the brightest from all of Asia. At its peak, it was home to 10,000 students and a faculty of 1,500. In the late twelfth century, Muslim armies swept down on Nalanda. The monks were butchered, and their libraries, with a staggering wealth of handwritten manuscripts, were torched.

According to the Dalai Lama, without these scholars and practitioners of Nalanda, there would be no Tibetan Buddhism as we know it today. "Every important text which we learn by heart, these texts all written by Nalanda masters," the Dalai Lama had explained to me. "So the name of these mas-

A RIFLE IN THE BEDROOM

ters, especially Nagarjuna, the second-century Buddhist master, very close in our minds. They are something very real. We practice according to their texts."

Elaborating on the Buddha's insights, Nagarjuna expounded a theory of reality grounded in the idea of the interdependence of all things. The Dalai Lama, over several decades, absorbed the essentials of the concept thoroughly. Interdependence conditions both the way he acts and the way he looks at life.

*I*NTERDEPENDENCE IS NOT the easiest of ideas to grasp. The Dalai Lama had used his vision of a peaceful coexistence with the Chinese to explain it to me. Now that I had accompanied him to Nalanda to pay homage to Nagarjuna, I wanted him to elaborate on the concept. As usual, Lhakdor, his monk translator, was with us.

Before he began, the Dalai Lama untied his shoelaces, carefully put his brown oxfords aside, and folded his legs into a lotus position on his chair. He would stay like this for the entire two-hour session. Interdependence is one of his favorite topics, and he relished the prospect of discussing it at length.

"The theory of interdependence allows us to develop a wider perspective," the Dalai Lama said. "With wider mind, less attachment to destructive emotions like anger, therefore more forgiveness. In today's world, every nation heavily interdependent, interconnected. Under these circumstances,

117

destroying your enemy—your neighbor—means destroying yourself in the long run. You need your neighbor. More prosperity in your neighbor, you'll get benefit.

"Now, we're not talking about the complete removal of feelings like anger, attachment, or pride. Just reduction. Interdependence is important because it is not a mere concept; it can actually help reduce the suffering caused by these destructive emotions.

"We can say the theory of interdependence is an understanding of reality," the Dalai Lama continued. "We understand that our future depends on global well-being. Having this viewpoint reduces narrow-mindedness. With narrow mind, more likely to develop attachment, hatred. I think this is the best thing about the theory of interdependence—it is an explanation of the law of nature. It affects profoundly, for example, the environment."

Interdependence is a fundamental principle in both Buddhism and ecology. The core belief is that all things are connected in some unfathomable but tangible way. Ultimately, all things are dependent on one another. We are all enmeshed in Indra's Net.

I flashed on something I'd once read about Charles Darwin. In a whimsical interlude, he had theorized that cat-loving spinsters made London one of the most pleasant places in the world to live. This was how his reasoning went. The large number of cats kept by these women had an adverse effect on the proliferation of mice. This was good news for the bumblebees—their underground nests were less likely to be destroyed by marauding mice. More bumblebees in turn caused more flowers to be pollinated. Therefore, Darwin came to the conclusion that more cat-loving English spinsters equals more flowers in London.

Expressing a similar insight, the Vietnamese Buddhist master Thich Nhat Hanh once wrote: "If you are a poet, you will see that there is a cloud in this sheet of paper. Without a cloud, there will be no rain; without rain, the trees cannot grow; and without trees, we cannot make paper."

Over the years, I've noticed that the Private Office of the Dalai Lama is very parsimonious with its paper stash. Whenever I receive some documents from them, they are invariably printed on the blank sides of used paper. His Holiness' private secretaries are fanatics about recycling paper, scrupulous about not offending the ecological sensibilities of their boss.

I can imagine the Dalai Lama putting this modest effort to save trees in the context of interdependence. His Private Office, over the past decades, has managed to save a few trees through their recycling efforts. More trees make for a better habitat for other plant life and for flowers. More trees, plants, and flowers create serendipitous conditions for poets, and poets living in serendipitous environment tend to produce more and richer poetry. This increased output ensures that bookstores specializing in poetry are well stocked. Because the Dalai Lama wants to save paper, poetry lovers everywhere have benefited.

I interrupted my reverie about Darwin, poets, and flowers

to ask the Dalai Lama: "How did you develop your under-standing of interdependence?"

"With time, with time," he replied. "Spiritual progress takes time. It's not like switching on a light. More like kin-dling a fire: start from small spark, then becomes bigger and bigger, more light, more light, like that. All mental transfor-mations like that. Not: up to certain stage, up to certain date, dark . . . then put on light. Not like that. Gradual, gradual. At beginning, not noticeable. Often I tell people: spiritual de-velopment—we cannot see results within weeks or months. Even years. But if we make comparison, today's experience compared to ten years ago, or twenty years ago, then you feel some change. That I always tell other people. My own case also like that."

"What is your present situation?" I asked.

"Since I meditate on or analyze interdependence for many years, now it is already familiar," the Dalai Lama replied. "So therefore, when I look at things, as soon as I remember the truth of interdependence, the picture becomes clearly differ-ent. And the sensation comes without much effort—almost au-tomatically. One example: in Mongolia, the big gathering . . ." He trailed off into Tibetan.

"His Holiness was in Ulan Bator," Lhakdor translated. "During teachings, when he reflected on interdependence, he saw the lack of tangibility in all these people before him and in himself—nothing was solid, everything was inter-twined. He had the strong sensation that he was connected directly to the audience in some way. It was as if his personal boundaries had dissolved."

The Dalai Lama's experience reminded me of the work of Andrew Newberg and Eugene d'Aquili, two American scientists who have studied the relationship between religious experience and brain function for many years. In their most celebrated experiment, they enlisted the help of an advanced meditator, a young American Buddhist called Robert. Inside a darkened lab, Robert began a meditation session with his little finger tied to a long coil of twine. The scientists, waiting in another room, held the other end.

One hour later, Robert tugged on the twine to let Newberg and d'Aquili know that he had entered a deep state of meditation. A radioactive tracer was then injected into his veins via an IV drip. The dye entered his bloodstream, infused his brain cells, and a high-tech camera gave the scientists a freeze-frame snapshot of Robert's brain activities. The scientists saw something unusual: Robert's posterior superior parietal lobe, dubbed the "orientation association area," or OAA, showed markedly reduced activity at the height of his meditation.

In our brains, the OAA acts as a gyroscope, radar, and GPS device all rolled into one. As we move about in our daily routines, the OAA functions like a supercomputer, continuously calculating the ever-shifting coordinates of our bodies in relation to everything around us. It allows us to negotiate our way safely through a crowded restaurant and to ride our bikes through traffic.

From their past research, Newberg and d'Aquili knew that the OAA never quits. So why this decrease in activity in Robert's OAA? Only one explanation made sense: sensory input into Robert's OAA was blocked when he reached a transcendent state during his meditation. With no data to feed it, the supercomputer had a hard time delineating Robert's physical boundaries. It had no choice but to conclude that Robert *had* no boundaries, that he was one with everything around him: people, things, the whole works.

When Robert was asked later what he felt during this climactic moment in his meditation, he replied, "It feels like I'm part of everyone and everything in existence. I'm connected to everything." It was precisely what spiritual masters and yogis had been saying for centuries. And it was remarkably similar to what the Dalai Lama had just told me: when he focuses on interdependence, he sees the world differently— things and people appear to lack solidity; edges soften and physical boundaries between him and others become blurred during these times of spiritual lucidity. Because of this, the Dalai Lama experiences a much deeper connection between himself and others.

"You've told me you're able to go into an experience of interdependence merely by thinking about it," I said to the Dalai Lama. "So, for example, take you and me. When you think about interdependence, do I change in a subtle way before your eyes?"

"Still human being, but then . . . not as it appears, not something solid. So something soft. Connection between us stronger, compassion is reinforced," the Dalai Lama replied. He thought for a moment, then spoke again to Lhakdor in Tibetan.

"Through this understanding of interconnected reality," Lhakdor translated, "you come to realize that if good things happen to others, you will also benefit; if not immediately, then eventually. If they suffer, you eventually suffer. Therefore, you are better able to empathize, even with people from very different backgrounds. Compassion for them comes easier."

"For example, Saddam Hussein," the Dalai Lama continued. "I get the feeling in the eyes of President [George W.] Bush, Saddam is one hundred percent negative, solidly negative. Only way is elimination. But reality not like that."

"What is the reality?" I asked.

"I think two levels. In conventional level, Saddam Hussein not one hundred percent wicked from birth—not something unchangingly bad." The Dalai Lama's hands circled each other, shaping an invisible sphere. "That wickedness comes from many other factors, not only from him. Therefore not independent. It is dependent on many other factors, including Americans themselves. During the Gulf Wars, everybody blamed Saddam Hussein. That I felt unfair, and my heart went out to him."

The Dalai Lama's heart went out to Saddam Hussein? To someone who had brought disaster to millions of people? This highlighted a singular truth about the Dalai Lama. His worldview, the way his mind works—however rational and inspiring they may be—is very different from mine.

"Saddam Hussein's dictatorship did not come out from the sky by itself," the Dalai Lama explained. "Saddam Hussein: dictator, invader, bad." He ticked off the points on his fingers, his expression grave. "But bad things happened because of his army. Without his army, without his weapons, he cannot be that kind of aggressor. These weapons not produced by Iraqis themselves, but come from West. Western companies helped to produce this aggressor. They did it, but afterward they blame on that person. Unfair." The Dalai Lama leaned far out of his chair; his voice rose a notch. He was getting worked up about this.

"So here, that's conventional level. Saddam Hussein not one hundred percent bad," he said. "Then more subtle level: when someone like Bush got some negative feelings toward Saddam Hussein, then in his eyes, Hussein is something solid, independent, absolute—totally bad." He extended a clenched fist in front of him and glared at it.

"Similarly, in Saddam Hussein's eyes . . ." The Dalai Lama started to giggle; he was having trouble finishing what he wanted to say. "Bush is something very negative. Absolute, independent . . . embodiment of evil." His words were now punctuated by loud hoots, his shoulders jiggling up and down uncontrollably. The Dalai Lama was getting a kick out of poking fun at the world's most powerful man.

When his laughter subsided, he concluded: "So, in both cases, strong misunderstanding of reality. This reality is mere mental projection."

"You're saying Saddam Hussein is not one hundred percent

solidly wicked because, for example, he might still be nice to his wife?" I asked the Dalai Lama.

"Oh, yes, yes," the Dalai Lama agreed enthusiastically. He was glad I had got the gist of his idea. "If circumstances changed, that person can become very nice person. Very possible. Another example. In [Osama] bin Laden's eyes, America one hundred percent evil. This ignorance brings disaster. To bin Laden, the entire West anti-Muslim. America in particular, aggressor of world. So he decides there is this solid, independent enemy. This is wrong view of reality."

"What should his view of reality be?" I asked.

"America is part of Arab; America is part of him," the Dalai Lama replied without hesitation.

"Interdependent," I said.

"Yes, interdependent. And not only America. In Western Europe, there's some criticism about Muslim there. But America and Europe not one hundred percent anti-Muslim. Of course not. So mental projection again. This is narrow focusing. Mistake. So interdependent view: wider now, soft. Not that solid thing to hold on to. This perspective reduces strong grasping, strong attachment—because there is no object to be strongly grasped. Our desire, our craving about things and people is reduced."

Through decades of sustained practice, the timeless truth of interdependence is seared into the Dalai Lama's consciousness. It has shaped his thoughts, beliefs, and behavior. He begins his projects, reacts to world events through the calculus of interdependence. He is not afraid to buck popular opinion. His decisions are not arrived at by the consensus of advisers or by opinion polls. His sympathy, or, at the very least, his lack of ill will, toward Saddam Hussein is the result of his special way of seeing, refracted through the prism of interdependence.

There is something else at work here too. The Dalai Lama had the impression that the United States and its allies were ganging up on the Iraqi dictator and his backward citizens subsisting in the desert. The Tibetan leader is congenitally sympathetic to the underdog, perhaps because of the compassionate influence of interdependence. I got an inkling of this in an earlier session with him when I was allowed to spend some time with him early in the morning in his Dharamsala residence.

Taking a break from his meditation, the Dalai Lama got up from his cushion and offered to show me his quarters. We walked out of his tranquil inner sanctum into a vestibule that led to the large, airy living room. Holding my hand, he led me into a small, sparsely furnished room opening off the vestibule. A small single bed took up much of the wood-paneled space; a lamp with a lotus-shaped shade and a portable radio were on a bedside table.

"This my old bedroom," the Dalai Lama told me. "Because of some earthquake warnings last year, I moved to another room in the basement."

He pointed out half a dozen faded photos on one wall. Nearly all were portraits of Tibetan monks, teachers he has had in his lifetime. In a rare photo of his beloved, now deceased senior tutor, Ling Rinpoche, the famously stern taskmaster actually had a slight smile on his face. In one corner of the room was a group picture of the Dalai Lama's entire family: his brothers and sisters and him together with their parents.

Then, on one end wall, I saw something out of place, even jarring. Just above the Dalai Lama's bed was a rifle. It hung vertically by its leather strap. I had my camera with me, and I prepared to take a photo of this incongruous item.

"No, no, no, don't take picture," the Dalai Lama hurriedly stopped me. "People might get the wrong idea that the Dalai Lama is someone violent, gun-loving." I put the camera down obediently. But I had an uneasy, nagging thought: since when does the Dalai Lama care what other people think? This behavior was surprising, so contrary to the Dalai Lama I had come to know. The Dalai Lama as a man of contradictions?

The Dalai Lama went on to tell me that he had had the air rifle for decades. "I often feed small birds, but when they come, hawks come also. This I don't like. Big hawks eating small birds. So, to protect these small living things, I keep the air rifle. Not to hurt, but just to scare them away."

9.

A Sea of Golden Turtles

It was the fifteenth day of the Tibetan month, traditionally a time for renewal. The Dalai Lama was in the small town of Bodhgaya to pay respects to Buddhism's holiest shrine. After a few days of much-needed rest here, he would continue with his pilgrimage and go to Vultures' Peak before returning to give the Kalachakra Initiation. The Dalai Lama mounted his throne inside the Mahabodhi Temple, beneath the shadow of the ancient bodhi tree, a direct descendent of the original tree under which the Buddha achieved enlightenment two and a half millennia ago. A large crowd of Tibetan monks sat facing him in the open courtyard. They were here to participate in the bimonthly ritual of *sojong*—confession.

As the monks began to chant, the Dalai Lama folded his body neatly into a Z-shaped bundle. From a kneeling position, he collapsed his legs so that his buttocks were resting on his heels. He then bent his upper body forward and down until his forehead touched the ground just in front of his knees, assuming a posture of pure humility. Because his body is so flexible from decades of sitting in the lotus position, he managed to accordion himself into the most compact form possible. With his yellow patchwork robe stretched across his back, he looked like a large golden turtle amid a sea of others.

It was the first time I had had the privilege of witnessing this most private of rituals, and I was awed. It was all the more remarkable because it was held in the very place where the Buddha became enlightened, with the Dalai Lama in attendance. Furthermore, monks from all four schools of Tibetan Buddhism were represented. It was a highly auspicious moment. After some time, a monk raised his head tentatively—one bald head in a field of gold. He took a quick, furtive look around, then tucked his head back down.

When I had the chance later, I asked the Dalai Lama what went through his mind during the sojong ritual. He told me: "I remembered the Buddha and all those great masters—like Nagarjuna—who visited Bodhgaya."

"Did you also make confessions?" I asked.

"Of course. Sojong means confession."

"What did you confess?"

"Eating biscuits in the evening," the Dalai Lama said. "As a Buddhist monk, I'm not supposed to eat anything after my midday meal."

AFTER THE CONCLUSION of the sojong ritual, the Dalai Lama got up and walked into the bodhi tree enclosure, a sacred precinct surrounded by thick stone fences. Five or six impossibly heavy branches jutted out horizontally from the magnificent tree. Industrial-grade iron posts, painted a dark green and cemented directly into the ground, kept the branches from drooping further and damaging the priceless, intricately carved stone fence. Silk-offering scarves had been flung up to the branches, along with strings of multicolored Tibetan prayer flags. Two women's umbrellas, covered in yellow and black polka dots, had somehow made their way up to the juncture between branch and trunk, another symbolic offering.

Brushing a dense mass of prayer flags aside, the Dalai Lama ducked through a narrow passage between the stone fence and the bodhi tree's massive trunk. The lower portion of the tree was wreathed completely in maroon and saffron silks. Gold leaves affixed by worshippers shimmered above. An overhead brass canopy, strung with strands of twinkling Christmas lights, protected a large stone tablet called the Diamond Seat. The Dalai Lama knelt and touched his head to the ancient slab in homage.

The Diamond Seat was where the Buddha sat and meditated on emptiness 2,500 years ago. He attained enlightenment when he internalized a profound truth—that phenomena are essentially empty; they do not exist independently of their causes and conditions.

In many of his lectures and interviews, the Dalai Lama invariably brings up the subject of emptiness. He says over and over that everything that the Buddha taught can be reduced to the essential idea of fusing emptiness with compassion. This is the formula for happiness: Emptiness+Compassion=Happiness.

According to the Dalai Lama, we need to first achieve wisdom by seeing the world as it is. Wisdom implies clear vision. With wisdom, we could view everything around us clearly, without preconception. Our gaze penetrates the fog out there like a laser beam. To do this, we have to develop real insight into emptiness. And what is emptiness? Emptiness is just another way of saying that things are devoid of individual, inherent existence. It says that, in the final analysis, nothing—people, thoughts, cars—can exist independently on its own. It is an enlightened way of looking at the world around us. It highlights a subtle but ultimate truth: interdependence rather than independence defines our lives and everything around us. None of us is an island. The world is a vast web of intertwined events, people, and things. These linkages may be difficult to see, but they are real, always there, lurking just beneath the surface. Coinciding with developing wisdom, we need method. And what is this method? Just cultivate compassion.

Compassion I could deal with. Although I'm not very

good at applying the idea in real life, I can understand it quite well. But emptiness was a different matter. Although I knew it was of fundamental importance, and I have some layman-like understanding of the basic concept, I have difficulties with its more subtle interpretations. After all, through the ages, whole libraries have been written on this ancient, elusive idea—an idea that has real implications for our modern lives. Perhaps I was too hung up on semantics, with the simplistic, everyday meaning of the word. "Empty," according to the dictionary in my head, equals nothing. But for the Dalai Lama, everything in the world—things, people, animals, thoughts, emotions, objects, you name it—is empty. Because everything is intertwined, there is no independence. Because there is no independence, nothing exists in and of itself. I found that to be a pretty difficult concept to grasp.

DURING ONE OF our interviews, the Dalai Lama had told me: "According to Buddhist belief, unless you meditate on and experience emptiness thoroughly, directly, it is very difficult to eliminate your destructive emotions." Ngari Rinpoche, the Dalai Lama's youngest brother, was present at the session. For much of the time, he simply listened. But at that comment, he jumped in: "Victor doesn't like emptiness; he refuses to listen to me about it." The Dalai Lama found that bit of information hilarious.

"Rinpoche's making fun of me as usual," I told the Dalai Lama. "I'm very interested in emptiness. I hope to get an explanation from you so that even a layperson like me can understand."

"You've attended so many of my teachings," the Dalai Lama said immediately. "You came to Dharamsala so many times. And you recorded every word I said. How come you now expect even more? Hopeless student."

But I wasn't the only one. I knew for a fact that Oprah Winfrey also had trouble with emptiness.

In May 2001, I had accompanied the Dalai Lama on a whirlwind tour of the United States, visiting nine cities in twenty-one days. A highlight of the tour was the Dalai Lama's meeting with U.S. President George W. Bush. That occasion stuck in my mind not because of what the two men discussed (it was more a courtesy call than anything substantial) but because of the Dalai Lama's footwear: he wore his usual Indian-made plastic flip-flops to the White House.

After his meeting with the president, the Dalai Lama went back to his hotel. Oprah was waiting for him. Accompanying her was a small army of photographers, makeup artists, and senior editors from O, *The Oprah Magazine,* her immensely successful magazine. They were ushered into the Dalai Lama's elegant suite for an in-depth interview.

The hour-long session began well enough. Oprah started by asking the Dalai Lama: "Have you ever had to forgive yourself for anything?"

"Small incidents, like accidentally killing an insect," the Dalai Lama replied.

"Killing an insect," Oprah said. "An insect . . . hmm. Okay."

The Dalai Lama continued, "My attitude toward mosquitoes is not very favorable, not very peaceful. Bed bugs also."

"And that's *it?*" Oprah couldn't quite believe what she was hearing. "In your lifetime, that's what you have to forgive yourself for?"

"Small mistakes every day, maybe," the Dalai Lama said evenly. "But major mistakes, it seems no."

"No major mistakes," Oprah repeated, mulling over the idea. She fell silent and looked out the window.

There was awe in her voice when she finally continued: "You have nothing in life that you have regrets about. That's a good life . . . that's a great life, to have no regrets."

"Regarding service to Tibet," the Dalai Lama said, "service to Buddhism, service to humanity . . . I have done as much as I can. Regarding my own spiritual practice, when I share my experiences with more advanced meditators—even those who have spent years in the mountains, practicing single-pointedness of mind—I don't lag too far behind."

"Would you encourage the rest of the world to meditate?" Oprah asked.

"Stupid question." The Dalai Lama's response was as immediate as it was unexpected.

Oprah's face froze. There was a stunned silence in the

hotel room. One thought crossed everyone's mind: this was probably the first time someone had ever said this to Oprah's face.

The Dalai Lama grew thoughtful. "Should people meditate? I think so," he said after a pause. Maybe it had been a stupid question, but he still wanted to reply with care. "It is worthwhile for the world to look more inward. We are not doing enough here. I'm not saying that people should be religious-minded. I'm not saying that. What I'm saying is: we should focus on our inner potential more."

"Oh, I believe that!" Oprah said, visibly relaxing. "That's why I asked the stupid question." Everyone in the room cracked up. "I wanted you to say it, but I certainly believe that."

"Of course it is not something we can impose on others. They have to adopt it voluntarily," the Dalai Lama went on.

But now that the tension had been dissipated, Oprah wanted to change the subject.

"In my magazine, I do a column called 'What I Know for Sure,'" Oprah said. "What do you know for sure? The one thing which you have no doubt."

The Dalai Lama did not hesitate. "Compassion is the best source of happiness—for happy life and happy world. There is no doubt."

"That what we give to others is going to come back. I agree with that."

"That is good . . . lots of agreement." The Dalai Lama laughed. "Although different cultures, different ideas, different ways of life. But we are same human being."

"When you say 'human being,' you mean we're of the same mind?"

"That's more complicated," the Dalai Lama replied. "Without investigating, everybody talks about human being, human being. But if we analyze what's human being, we cannot find."

"We can't?"

"That's a Buddhist concept—emptiness. Emptiness does not mean nothing exists. Things exist, but the way they exist, we cannot find. Therefore empty."

"Ahhh . . ." Oprah pondered that bit of wisdom.

The Dalai Lama continued: "So emptiness means this vase," he gestured to a flower container on the coffee table, "it exists, but it is the way of existence that we cannot find. Therefore empty. Empty nature."

I got the sense that the Dalai Lama wanted to give his interviewer a fuller explanation of emptiness. But Oprah hesitated. "That's going to be hard to explain to my readers," she told him. She started to ask the Dalai Lama about his childhood in Tibet instead.

In the August 2001 issue of O, *the Oprah Magazine*, Oprah's readers were treated to a beguiling, in-depth cover story about the Dalai Lama. But there was not a word about emptiness. However, a few months after Oprah's interview, I got to learn more about this elusive concept in the small pilgrimage town of Bodhgaya, India.

10.

A Korean Scholar in Bodhgaya

The famous Korean scholar, dressed impeccably in a black, faux Confucian gown with high collar and long, flowing sleeves, sat cross-legged before the Dalai Lama.

It was early January 2002. We were seated on cushions covered with Tibetan fabric in the Dalai Lama's quarters on the top floor of the Tibetan Monastery, his temporary home during his stay in Bodhgaya. I was feeling slightly peeved. I was supposed to have at least two interviews here with the Dalai Lama, before I accompanied him to the pilgrimage site of Vultures' Peak. But the scholar, Kim Yong-Oak, Harvard-educated and host of a popular Korean TV show on Confucius, had managed to arrange an audience the day before. He had apparently impressed the Dalai Lama so much that he had been granted another interview that day. I had had one session two days earlier, and it looked like that was all I was going to get.

"This may be a very silly question . . ." the Korean said hesitatingly as he started his interview with the Dalai Lama. He took off his black brimless hat, one that resembled an American sailor's cap, revealing a shaven head. I guessed that he was in his early fifties. "Throughout your life," the scholar continued, his words running together, "you have studied so much and disciplined your body so much. And you have had all kinds of experiences. You're a great thinker. Can you tell me something personal in your life, some enlightenment experience?"

I was surprised by the question. It was personal and impertinent, especially on only a second meeting. Still, I was interested in the answer. Would the Dalai Lama reveal something deeply personal to this virtual stranger, discuss something that great religious masters rarely talk about? Would he recount his experience of spiritual awakening?

The Dalai Lama leaned back on his cushion, his expression grave.

"This body, now sixty-six years old. But my spiritual level, I'm very young," the Tibetan monk said. He paused to laugh uproariously at his own joke, his whole body shaking. "But of course, the concept of impermanence, and also the concept of emptiness, very powerful. Very useful," he said, growing thoughtful. "Especially the concept of emptiness." Kim took out a notepad and started scribbling.

"According to Nagarjuna, emptiness means interdependency or interconnectedness," the Dalai Lama said as he leaned toward the Korean. Nagarjuna was the second-century Indian master whose teachings provided the foundation for Tibetan Buddhism.

"Emptiness does not mean nothingness," the Dalai Lama continued. "Emptiness is full, not empty. The realization of emptiness, knowledge of emptiness . . . I think I have some intellectual understanding. Emptiness—you can also think of it as interdependence—helps us widen our view. Our view toward the world, our view toward one's own life. It really widens. It is very helpful to develop this holistic view."

The Dalai Lama looked away from the Korean and spoke briefly in Tibetan to Lhakdor, his translator.

"Coffee or tea?" Lhakdor, sitting on the floor next to the Tibetan, asked the scholar.

"Anything. Er . . . tea."

"Maybe coffee," the Dalai Lama prompted helpfully.

"Yeah, coffee . . ."

"One Korean, Americanized by Harvard," the Dalai Lama joked.

"Okay, tea," the Korean responded. "Yes, maybe I'm too Americanized. But even though I received my education in a foreign country, I am regarded as a most traditional man in Korea."

"That's very good. Very good." The Dalai Lama nodded.

"These are just clothes I designed myself," Kim said, patting his sleek, black gown. "But usually I wear very traditional clothes. Never Western clothes."

Kim had brought along two photographers and a secretary to the interview. One of the young men had been quietly snapping pictures from the side. Kim now turned away from the Dalai Lama and spoke briefly to the photographer, who then moved behind the Tibetan monk so that he could better focus on his boss.

The Dalai Lama was eager to go on with the interview. "Now, emptiness and compassion," he told the Korean, paying no attention to the camera flashes. "Of course, firstly, we understand these ideas at an intellectual level. Also the positive sides of compassion and the destructiveness of selfishness. Then, eventually, there is impact on our emotions. Our emotions slowly change. That's the Buddhist way. Use reason, make use of intellect. So, regarding compassion and understanding emptiness, I have a little experience. That experience certainly brought benefit. Great benefit. I have full conviction, now that I have this small experience, that if I practice further, even greater benefits will come to me. It's guaranteed. You develop these qualities, you'd acquire peace and happiness."

"Your Holiness, can you tell me something about emptiness?" the Korean asked. I was glad that he, like Oprah and me, had difficulty with the concept.

"There are two levels of reality," the Dalai Lama explained to his Korean visitor. "One level of reality: you see this is a table." He passed his left hand lightly over the low table between the two of them. Then he pointed to his mug of hot water, his preferred drink at all times of the day: "This is water."

"Conventional reality," the Korean said.

"Now, how to prove the existence of this conventional reality?" the Dalai Lama said as he moved the mug directly in front of him. "This water exists. I see, I feel . . . this is water." He leaned closer to the table, peered into the mug, and jabbed a forefinger at it a couple of times for emphasis. He took off his glasses and bent forward at the waist, until his face was just inches above the mug. "On second look, still water."

The Dalai Lama straightened up, put his glasses back on, and pointed to Lhakdor, seated on the carpet to his right. "Ask someone else, yes, still water. Then we accept it: this is real."

"You talk about conventional truth," Kim Yong-Oak said.

"Yes, conventional truth. But let's say, all of a sudden, I saw fruit juice. Instead of water, I saw this mug filled with fruit juice—yellow." The Dalai Lama took off his glasses again. He wiped his eyes with the back of his hand and bent toward the mug once more. "Then I look carefully: all I see is water. So this proves the first perception was wrong—seeing the yellow color was a mistake. When I take a closer look, the fruit juice was not there."

The Dalai Lama put his glasses back on and studied the Korean for a moment to see if any of this had sunk in. He was saying that our everyday perception can be suspect. Physical defects, like tricky lighting conditions, can make us see things incorrectly.

"Another example. Due to my color blindness, I always see black." He pointed to the mug and said to the scholar, "Today

147

I see black mug, and this afternoon also see black mug. But then I cannot be sure. I ask someone: 'Look, what's this color?' If that person confirms this is black, then it's conventionally confirmed: this is black."

He pointed to Lhakdor and the two photographers who had accompanied the scholar to the audience. "But if second person, third person, fourth person say, 'This is yellow,' then, although I always see this as black, something wrong with my eyes. Reality is not black. It is in this way I always try to find the truth, the conventional truth—through rational investigation."

The Dalai Lama was expounding on something dear to his heart: a scientific, no-nonsense view of the world. He had no use for wishy-washy, half-baked ideas. After all, this was a man who had studied logic intensively for more than a decade in his youth. What he was trying to explain was this: most of us attach meaning and significance to everything as a way of understanding and interpreting our world. But our experiences influence how we see the world. To apprehend things without distortion, we need to investigate them with scientific rigor.

"Now let's look at ultimate reality," the Dalai Lama said, pointing a little finger to his mug. "What exactly is it?" The Dalai Lama leaned very close to the Korean scholar and stared at him intently. "We're seeing color, shape. But if we take away shape, color, material, what is mug? Where is the mug? This mug is a combination of particles: atoms, electrons, quarks. But each particle not 'mug.' The same can be said about the four elements, the world, everything. The Buddha. We cannot find the Buddha. So that's the ultimate reality. If we're not satisfied with conventional reality, if we go deep down and try to find the real thing, we ultimately won't find it."

Thus, the Dalai Lama was saying, the mug is empty. The term "mug" is merely a label, something we use to describe everyday reality. But each mug comes into existence because of a complex web of causes and conditions. It does not exist independently. It cannot come into being by itself, of its own volition.

For example: suppose I decide to make a black mug. To do this, I mix black clay and water, shape it to my liking, and fire the resulting mixture in an oven. Clay plus water turns into a mug because of my actions. But it exists because of the myriad different ways that atoms and molecules interact. And what about me, the creator of the black mug? If my parents had never met, the black mug might never have existed.

Therefore the mug does not exist independently. It comes into being only through a complex web of relationships. In the Dalai Lama's own words, and this is the key concept in his worldview, the mug is "dependently originated." It came to be a mug because of a host of different factors, not under its own steam. It is empty. "Empty" is shorthand for "empty of intrinsic, inherent existence." Or to put it another way, empty is another word for interdependent.

The Dalai Lama's eyes never left the Korean's face. I was

struck by the intensity of his gaze. The photographers' clumsy movement around him and the loud clicks of the shutters had no discernable effect on him.

Why should we care about emptiness? What has it got to do with our real lives? For the Dalai Lama, perspective is everything. Much of our unhappiness, our suffering, is caused by discrepancies between our perceptions and what is real. For example, I see myself as a distinct entity: I am different from my daughter, my wife, my enemy. Whether I love these people or hate them, I believe that I exist independently from them. Due to my lifelong conditioning, there is no doubt in my mind that there is a sharp distinction between myself and others. The idea of self-interest, of every person for themselves, makes sense from this perspective.

However, if I accept the Dalai Lama's point of view, I see that my existence depends on an infinite, intricately linked series of events, people, causes, and conditions. If any of these things had been different, I would exist in different ways. If my parents had been born in Lhasa, I'd likely be a Tibetan rather than Chinese. If I hadn't been kidnapped in Afghanistan in 1972, I might not have met the Dalai Lama.

From this perspective, "self" and "others" make sense only in terms of relationships. For the Dalai Lama, the essence, the crux of reality, is the fundamental interconnectedness between people and people, and between people and things. This is how he views the world around him. For well over half a century, he has believed, in the core of his being, that "his" interest and "your" interest are inextricably connected. In a

very tangible way, they intersect. And that is why he has devoted his entire life to the well-being of others. He calls it enlightened self-interest. He is convinced that if he can be of
help to others, he himself will be the first to benefit—he'll be
a happier man as a result. He has no higher calling than this.

The interview came to a close. For about an hour, the
Dalai Lama had patiently explained to Kim Yong-Oak how
he himself was transformed in baby steps, over the years, by
using a sensible, logical approach to his spiritual practice. He
underscored the importance of reason. He was emphatic that
anyone could achieve genuine happiness by focusing on two
fundamental precepts of Buddhism: compassion and emptiness. But in the end, the Dalai Lama chose not to talk about
his own enlightenment experiences with the Korean scholar.

11.

Some Positive, Invisible Vibrations

The Dalai Lama left his simple quarters on the top floor of the Tibetan Monastery in Bodhgaya and walked down two flights of exterior stairs to the cramped monastery courtyard. The white Ambassador was parked there. It looked just like any other scruffy taxi found in Indian cities. But this one was heavily armor-plated, its thick, tinted windows strong enough to deflect bullets. A small group of radical Maoists had been agitating near Bodhgaya in recent months. And this part of Bihar, the poorest state in India, was known for the occasional armed robbery. The Foreign Office in Delhi had the car shipped from the nearby city of Lucknow for the Dalai Lama to use during his pilgrimage to Bodhgaya and other nearby Buddhist sites.

The Dalai Lama walked past the car and out of the

monastery, accompanied by an entourage of about fifty people: his aides and attendants; some high lamas; an assortment of Indian and Tibetan security guards. The area outside the monastery, the epicenter of Bodhgaya, had been cleared. A large crowd of pilgrims and well-wishers waiting patiently to catch a glimpse of the revered Tibetan leader were confined to the sidewalks. The police had allowed no cars or bicycle rickshaws on the streets.

The Dalai Lama relished this short walk to the sacred Mahabodhi Temple, the site where the Buddha attained enlightenment. It would give him a chance to interact with ordinary people. From time to time, he darted away from his bodyguards to greet someone in the crowd.

A small army of beggars, mostly women of indeterminate age in colorful saris, sat on their haunches outside the temple gates. They were the untouchables of India, and they had traveled long distances to Bodhgaya, in time for the 2002 Kalachakra Initiation—an eleven-day Tibetan Buddhist ritual to be performed by the Dalai Lama in front of 200,000 people. "Here in Bodhgaya," the Dalai Lama had explained to me, "such a large number of people will come together for a few days to concentrate on altruism. Because of this, I think some positive vibrations, perhaps at an invisible level, can happen. But I can assure you, no matter whether positive or not, at least no harm. And I think the participants, for some short moments, can experience some tranquility, some peace and satisfaction. That usually happens in Kalachakra Initiations."

One thing was certain. The beggars knew they wouldn't go hungry. And they knew that, at the end of the two-week extravaganza, each of them would likely be able to go home with a tidy wad of rupees.

The beggars took little notice of the approaching Dalai Lama. Instead, their attention was intently focused on the half-dozen Tibetans lugging a large aluminum bucket of saffron rice toward them. With quick, practiced movements, two young men ladled generous portions into the proffered tin cups. This ritual was enacted twice a day. Scampering on their hands and knees alongside the fast-moving Tibetans were five or six crippled boys, their matchstick legs waving rhythmically behind their skinny bodies like tails. The boys also would not go hungry—not while the Dalai Lama was in town.

At the entrance to the temple's inner sanctum, the Dalai Lama slipped off his plastic flip-flops and prostrated three times on a crimson silk blanket laid on the floor by his attendant. He then walked through a narrow passage into a small chapel dominated, at the far end, by a large statue of the Buddha.

The Dalai Lama approached the throne, the statue towering above him. He prostrated three more times. A group of Sri Lankan monks, resplendent in their bright saffron robes, hovered nearby. They are the official guardians of the temple. A dozen high Tibetan lamas in maroon robes and a handful of Tibetan bodyguards were the only other people in the small room. The air was close, pungent with the heavy, sweet smell of incense and the sour, lingering body odor of count-less worshippers.

I stood wedged next to Senge Rabten, the Dalai Lama's chief bodyguard. The short, crew-cut karate expert got on his tiptoes and tried to adjust a wall-mounted fan. After some fumbling, he succeeded in directing a stream of stale air in the direction of the Dalai Lama. I could hear the sounds of the huge mob outside, kept in check by soldiers carrying auto-matic weapons.

One of the Sri Lankan monks handed a lighted tinder to the Dalai Lama. Two purple candles, spiral in shape and fit-ted on brass receptacles, stood on a ledge before the statue. The Dalai Lama lit them carefully, one after the other. He then looked up at the Buddha statue and raised his right hand in a gesture of homage.

I squinted at the ancient stone statue, said to have been sculpted some 1,700 years ago. When it was unearthed by nineteenth-century British archeologists, its head had been severed from its body. They cemented it back on before in-stalling the statue in the inner sanctum of the temple. I knew that when the Dalai Lama first laid eyes on this all-important image, he'd been disturbed to see the very visible joint. He made a sizable donation, requesting that the image be painted over in gold. The Archeological Survey of India protested, but in the end, religious sensibilities won out. The wall be-hind the statue was painted blue and bathed in soft light, giv-ing the effect of a large window framing perfect blue sky. I tried without success to pick out the telltale crease around the statue's neck.

The Dalai Lama walked back outside the chapel. He turned to his right and rounded the central tower of the temple.

Just before he reached the temple gates, he abruptly changed course and broke off to the right, approaching a large throng of Tibetans straining against the security personnel. With his bodyguard beside him, he headed for a young man seated on the ground next to an old woman with broad Mongolian features, her hair in two long plaits. The young man, in his early twenties, had a cane in his hand. Somehow, although his eyes were open, the Dalai Lama had surmised that he was blind. The Tibetan monk bent down, took the man's hand, and spoke to him in his deep baritone. He wanted to know where the blind man had come from, whether he had received any medical treatment. I marveled at the Dalai Lama's uncanny ability to pick out the disenfranchised, the disabled, from giant crowds.

I would later learn that the young man, Lobsang Thinley, had come with his mother from the Machen area of Amdo, part of the Chinese province of Qinghai in Northeast Tibet. He had lost his sight at the age of fifteen, when he suffered a severe concussion after a fall. An operation had restored his sight partially, but before long his blindness returned. Over the years, his mother had tried desperately to find a cure for her son, taking him to major hospitals in Chengdu and Beijing, where he had another operation and was also treated with acupuncture and moxibustion. Nothing worked. The man's optical nerves were badly damaged, and he was told that he would not see again.

When he heard that the Dalai Lama, for the first time in fifteen years, would perform the Kalachakra Initiation in Bodhgaya in early 2002, the son was determined to go. He wanted to be near the Dalai Lama, to hear his teachings. Family and friends tried to dissuade him: the journey from Northeast Tibet to Nepal and India through the Himalayas would be arduous and dangerous. But he refused to listen. His mother sold all her jewelry and cattle and borrowed from relatives to scrape together enough money for the trip. She still held out hope that her son would be cured one day. Maybe they might get lucky in India, the birthplace of Buddhism.

After a brief exchange with mother and son, the Dalai Lama turned to leave. The young man held on to his hands for a few more moments, reluctant to let go. The Dalai Lama spoke to one of his aides. He wanted Dr. Tseten Dorji Sadutshang, one of his personal doctors and the director of the Delek Hospital in Dharamsala, to examine the man to see if anything could be done. Then he left the Mahabodhi temple and walked back to the Tibetan Monastery.

12.

Like Molding Clay

A couple of days after the Dalai Lama's encounter with the blind man in Bodhgaya, I had dinner as usual in the small second-floor dining room of the Tibetan Monastery. All the members of the Dalai Lama's entourage, from the secretary of the Private Office to the bodyguards, ate their meals there. Most evenings, the fare was traditional Tibetan dishes of plain dumplings and noodle soup with vegetables.

As I started on the soup, Dr. Tseten Dorji Sadutshang slid in beside me. We'd first met two years earlier in Spiti, an ancient Tibetan kingdom north of Dharamsala. Dr. Tseten, as he is known, is intense and rail-thin. A permanent air of scholarly introspection clings to him, and he speaks in thoughtful and measured tones. He keeps mostly to himself, but he can be surprisingly gregarious at times.

I asked him about the blind man, Lobsang Thinley, from Tibet.

"I got the message from His Holiness," Dr. Tseten told me. "But before I could go and check on the blind man, someone came to me with a piece of news. A young Tibetan, a monk from the Drepung Monastery in South India, wanted to donate his eyes to the man."

I stopped slurping my noodle soup. I looked around the room to see if others had heard. But no one had taken any notice.

"Yes, it's amazing," the Harvard-educated doctor said. "I have never heard of such a thing before. Eye donations, yes, from dead people. But never from a living person."

"Are the two men related?" I asked, after a long pause.

"They met on pilgrimage in Sarnath, just before taking the train together to Bodhgaya. They knew each other for only a few days."

"Have you met the young blind man?" I asked.

"Yes, I went to the camp where the pilgrims from Tibet stay. There were two or three hundred people living in canvas tents just behind the temple. They had all managed to get through the Himalayas to Nepal and then bribed the border guards to let them into India. The blind man was in a tent together with eight or ten others. His mother cried the whole time I was there."

"Did you check his eyes?"

"No. It was impossible. The light was poor, and I didn't have any instruments with me."

"Did you tell him about the monk's offer?"

"He knew about it already. I told him that first he would have to have a thorough examination so that we could find out what's wrong with his eyes. And both men would need to be checked to see whether they were compatible, whether the transplant was possible."

I resumed eating my soup. Dr. Tseten stared into his own bowl of noodles. He had eaten very little of it.

"The blind man told me he had thought long and hard about the donation," he continued. "Of course he was tremendously moved. But he said in the end he had to refuse. He has suffered tremendously over the years, and he simply can't bear the thought of another person going through the same agony."

Dr. Tseten told me he had gone the next day to the camp where the monks from Drepung Monastery stayed. He wanted to meet Tsering Dhondup, the man who had offered to donate his eyes. The monk was not in.

"Yesterday, I went to see His Holiness and told him about the monk's offer," Dr. Tseten said.

"What was his reaction?"

"It was one of the most precious moments in my life," Dr. Tseten said quietly. "Even before I had finished telling him about the monk, I could feel this great outpouring of empathy, of compassion, welling up from deep within him. It was real, almost a physical thing. But he didn't say a word. My eyes started to tear up. I had never felt something like this before. Compassion so powerful, enveloping me, seeping into me."

OMPASSION IS A THEME the Dalai Lama returns to over and over again. I don't believe I have ever sat through one of his lectures or teachings without hearing him go on at length about it. I also know he has meditated on compassion every morning without fail for the past half century.

In an interview, I asked the Dalai Lama to give me his take on compassion. Lhakdor, as usual, was by his side.

"Compassion is something like a sense of caring, a sense of concern for others' difficulties and pain," the Dalai Lama said. "Not only family and friends, but all other people. Enemies also. Now, if we really analyze our feelings, one thing becomes clear. If we think only of ourselves, forget about other people, then our minds occupy very small area. Inside that small area, even tiny problem appears very big. But the moment you develop a sense of concern for others, you realize that, just like ourselves, they also want happiness; they also want satisfaction. When you have this sense of concern, your mind automatically widens. At this point, your own problems, even big problems, will not be so significant. The result? Big increase in peace of mind. So, if you think only of yourself, only your own happiness, the result is actually less happiness. You get more anxiety, more fear.

"So this is what I think of as the compassionate effect: if you really want genuine happiness, then whatever method you use to get it is worthwhile. And the best method is: when you think of others, you'll be the first to get maximum benefit."

I asked the Dalai Lama how he came by this understanding of compassion.

"I was thirty-two years old when I developed a strong experience of compassion," he told me. "In 1967, I received teaching of Shantideva's 'Bodhisattva's Way of Life' from a high lama. Since then I read and thought about compassion. My mind became close to it, my feeling about it very strong. Often when I reflect on the meaning and benefits of altruistic mind, tears came."

He turned to speak to Lhakdor in Tibetan. Lhakdor translated: "Based on his own understanding, the development of compassion had been ongoing since that time. When he meditated on compassion, he would sometimes be filled with joy and appreciation. And there is a strong sense of concern for others accompanied by a feeling of sadness."

"Is there another watershed in your development of compassion after 1967?" I asked the Dalai Lama.

"Continuous," he replied in English, before speaking to Lhakdor in Tibetan.

"In the late eighties, His Holiness' experience of compassion getting stronger and stronger," Lhakdor translated. I noticed that the Dalai Lama was reluctant to speak to me directly about his spiritual achievements. Perhaps he was concerned that he gave the impression of boasting. He was obviously more comfortable talking through Lhakdor.

"From that time, the sensation of compassion comes to you more easily?" I asked.

"Yes," the Dalai Lama said, adding something in Tibetan.

Lhakdor started to translate. "One thing: after developing this real experience with compassion, there were these frequent episodes of . . ."

"Conviction, more proper word," the Dalai Lama interrupted. "I cannot say 'real experience.' Strong conviction."

"An indication of that strong conviction," Lhakdor continued. "Whenever he meditated or reflected on compassion, it would lead to powerful emotions, lead to tears during some public teachings or private study. And when His Holiness reflected on certain profound explanations on emptiness, this would also trigger a strong emotion."

"I think that strong conviction or strong emotions actually give more inner strength," the Dalai Lama explained. "So when I face some problems or criticism, for example, sometime baseless criticism from the Chinese, of course, little irritation sometimes . . ."

"But then he'll have this feeling of compassion for them," Lhakdor translated. "He'll regret they're not making positive connection with him. But his sentiment is, although there is this negativity, may it also give positive fruit. Another thing: His Holiness wants to emphasize that his development of compassion is the result of long practice."

"Hard work," I offered.

"Not very hard work," the Dalai Lama said. "I think early

morning, I reflect on compassion, about few minutes. Some meditation, some analytic meditation. Of course, every morning, I take altruism vow. At that time, I reflect on compassion, recite some verses, till I get some kind of strong feeling.

"Now, the understanding of emptiness helps a lot toward developing compassion. There's no doubt it reinforces compassion," the Dalai Lama said, punching the air several times with his right index finger.

Lhakdor elaborated: "Emptiness allows us to have an understanding about ultimate reality. It helps us to appreciate the wisdom of interdependence—a fundamental law of nature. We gain an appreciation that we are all basically related. It is because of this interrelatedness that we are able to empathize with the suffering of others. With empathy, compassion flows naturally. We develop genuine sympathy for others' suffering and the will to help remove their pain. Emptiness thus strengthens positive emotions like compassion."

Emptiness and compassion. Wisdom and method. These are the twin pillars of the Dalai Lama's practice—everything we need to know about spiritual practice. He often uses a metaphor to illustrate their central importance. Just as a bird needs two wings to fly, a person with wisdom and no compassion is like a lonely hermit vegetating in the mountains; a compassionate person without wisdom is nothing more than a likable fool. Both qualities are needed; they strengthen each other. Once we realize we are all interconnected, it is

difficult not to feel some sense of compassion for the problems of our fellow human beings. And once we come by a
feeling of compassion, we start to get a glimpse of the timeless truth of interdependence, of emptiness.

The Dalai Lama looked thoughtful. After some time, he
turned to me, and his eyes sought mine. "I think one thing I'm
quite sure," he said. "I can tell you, the twin practice of emptiness and compassion is . . ." Then he lapsed into Tibetan
again.

Lhakdor translated. "His Holiness can say with conviction: if you meditate on emptiness and compassion, so long
as you make the effort, then His Holiness is sure that, day in
and day out, you will get tangible benefit. Your whole attitude will change."

"I think these two practices quite clever . . ." The Dalai
Lama trailed off, not entirely satisfied that "clever" was the
right word. He stared into space, his palms together in front
of his face. "I think . . . *effective*. I think understanding emptiness makes things soft, then compassion makes new shape."
At the end of his last sentence, he clashed his palms together
like cymbals.

"Like molding clay," Lhakdor volunteered.

"These things about compassion are something living—
according to my own experience," the Dalai Lama went on.
"I tell some of my experiences to other people, share some of
my feelings, then other people understand: there is something real, something living. Otherwise many people get im-

pression: these are something like Buddhist 'heaven'—just idea, just concept, not something living . . ."

"Almost like telling a fairy tale," Lhakdor translated, as the Dalai Lama rocked back and forth on his chair, his body racked with laughter.

13.

The Making of a Space Yogi

Five Indian commandos formed a human shield around the Dalai Lama as he trudged up the steep trail leading to Vultures' Peak, one of the key pilgrimage sites for Buddhists. These soldiers, members of an elite unit in the Indian army, were dressed immaculately in black: long-sleeved cotton shirts, flowing head scarves, and crisply pressed pants. Each had a second scarf tied around the lower part of his face so that only his eyes were visible. All carried automatic weapons. Two of them, specially trained sharpshooters, had precision rifles slung on their shoulders. Even without their weapons, the broad-shouldered men were impressive looking; each stood over six feet tall and was obviously immensely fit.

More soldiers, in khakis and blue berets, trailed behind. I

had never seen the Dalai Lama so well protected in India. It was a rare event for the Tibetan leader to be visiting this out-of-the-way pilgrimage site in Bihar, the poorest, most anarchic state of the country; the authorities were leaving nothing to chance.

The Dalai Lama climbed slowly but steadily, leaning with deliberation into a walking stick fashioned from a scrawny-looking branch. From time to time he chatted briefly with his Indian escorts, but mainly he kept to himself. A quarter of the way up, he took off his maroon outer shawl and handed it to Buchung, his attendant, who folded it carefully into a square packet. At one point, the Dalai Lama walked a few steps off the path to look at a small meditation cave dug into the side of the hill. A disciple of the Buddha had cloistered himself there in meditation two and a half millennia ago.

By the time we reached the top of Vultures' Peak, the Dalai Lama was sweating. He stopped, reached inside his monk's tunic, and pulled out a tissue, dabbing his forehead and face with it. Bowing slightly, Tenzin Taklha, close at hand as always, held out a hand for the used wipe. But the Dalai Lama put it back inside his tunic.

The top of Vultures' Peak was a handkerchief-sized piece of flat ground hemmed in by rocky outcrops on three sides. On the fourth, the knife-edged ridge dropped steeply down a valley. A U-shaped brick enclosure, built to waist height, dominated the flat area. Numerous offering candles had been placed on top of the enclosure's low walls.

After prostrations, the Dalai Lama walked to the edge of

the ridge and looked down onto the flat valley of Rajgir, three hours' drive from Bodhgaya. A lone red-dirt road bisected the verdant farmland, leading straight to the high mountains ringing the valley. The view was gorgeous. But the Dalai Lama didn't linger over it. His mind was on the prayers—the wisdom sutras explaining the concept of emptiness—that he had come to recite. It was on this spot that two and a half thousand years ago, the Buddha expounded the doctrine of emptiness, an idea that lies at the heart of Buddhist knowledge.

In previous meetings with me, the Dalai Lama had explained at length the interrelated concepts of interdependence and emptiness—they are the two sides of the same coin, two different ways to come to grips with the same idea. This is what he has told me: the existence of anything—coffee mugs, feelings of jealousy—is totally dependent on a complex web of relationships. Because of this, if you think about it long enough, there is no logical way for these things to exist independently. Therefore, in the Dalai Lama's terminology, they are said to be devoid of a life of their own. They have no inherent existence. In other words, they are empty. He had also told me that to fully appreciate these central concepts, to transcend mere intellectual understanding, a rigorous spiritual practice involving long periods of meditation is indispensable.

In another interview, I wanted to know how the Dalai Lama first encountered the concept of emptiness and how it has subsequently assumed such pivotal importance in his life.

"Emptiness is not an easy thing to understand," the Dalai Lama told me. "But once I developed some understanding, some direct insights, then I realized it is applicable to almost all experiences, all situations."

He turned to Lhakdor and spoke to him in Tibetan. "Having gained more knowledge with growing age, the influence of emptiness on his life becomes more pronounced," Lhakdor translated.

"I think around twenty years old, I already developed genuine interest in emptiness," the Dalai Lama continued, rocking backward and forward gently on the edge of his chair. "I remember one incident. In 1954, I attended the National People's Congress in Peking. There were some days without much engagements. So I asked to study emptiness with Ling Rinpoche, my senior tutor. That was one indication of my interest."

The Dalai Lama fell silent, his rhythmic rocking stopped. He sat ramrod straight and stared into the distance. After a few moments, he scratched his chin and started to speak again in Tibetan to Lhakdor, rubbing his right hand gently, in a circular motion, around his chest. Lhakdor leaned far forward, his eyes fixated on the Tibetan leader as he translated. "It was in His Holiness' late twenties, in 1963. One day he was reading a Buddhist text. At one point he came across a line which says: 'I' is merely designated to the self of physical aggregates (mental and physical collection). As soon as he read that, he got a special kind of sensation, a strange experience." Lhakdor's voice was a hoarse whisper; I had to strain to hear the words.

"How long did that strange experience last?" I asked.

"That feeling lasted, I think, few weeks, maybe," the Dalai Lama replied. He spoke to Lhakdor some more. The furrows on his brow lightened; he peered down at the floor in front of him and gestured to the carpet with a sweeping motion. There was a look of wonder on his face.

"During this time," Lhakdor translated, "whenever he saw people, things . . . carpet, for example, he would see them as carpet and people, but at the same time, he noticed that they have no essence. He had the distinct feeling that there is no 'I.' Not in the sense that 'I' do not exist, but a certain feeling of no 'I' as we understand it."

"Absence of solid reality," the Dalai Lama said emphatically. He raised both his hands to chest level and clenched them into tight fists.

"Did you have any visions?" I asked tentatively, unsure of the wisdom of pursuing this line of questioning. I had just realized that the conversation had taken an unexpected turn. The Dalai Lama was telling me something very personal, something perhaps only a handful of people had ever heard.

"No," he answered.

"But there was this experience of no 'I,' " I said.

"Yes."

The Dalai Lama again spoke directly to Lhakdor. "Physically, something like lightning surged through his heart,"

Lhakdor translated. "He experienced something like an electric shock."

I had the uncomfortable sensation that I was eavesdropping. Spiritual realizations are intimate, personal experiences for a Buddhist, and this was the first time I had ever heard a serious practitioner talk about them. But I needed to confirm what I'd just heard. "An electric shock going through your body?" I asked the Dalai Lama.

"Yes," he replied. He was watching me closely, his hands now clasped on his lap.

I heard a soft click, a sound that seemed to come from far away. Then I realized my tape recorder had stopped; the tape was finished. I kept my eyes fixed on the Dalai Lama, not trusting my ability to fish a new tape from my day pack. I'd get a copy of the interview from Lhakdor later.

"In those few weeks you saw objects as without essence, without substance?" I asked. The Dalai Lama sat very straight in his chair, his face impassive. It occurred to me that he looked very much like a Buddha at that moment. I couldn't help feeling awed by his presence.

"Yes. If I thought about non-self, no 'I,'" he elaborated, "then in that one moment, just like picture. I think it is similar to watching TV or a movie. It is especially like watching a movie. One way to look at the movie: feeling something real going on in there. But at the same time, while your eyes looking there, your mind knows this is mere picture—acting, not real. So seeing same picture: one, without understanding this is acting; another, seeing but still feel this is acting."

The Dalai Lama was telling me that his way of seeing had changed after the strange experience of 1963. He saw that things now appeared to have two facets. One: solid, real, touchable, the kind of everyday things we encountered—fridge, anger, neighbors. Second: the underlying unreal nature of things—things that are like a picture show—their essences nothing but flickering Technicolor mirages on a wide screen. Their existence, characterized by constant change and impermanence, depends on a web of relationships. All things—fridge, anger, neighbors—can be viewed in these two perspectives.

The influence of the 1963 incident stayed with him, the Dalai Lama told me. As he continued with his practice and meditated on a daily basis, his spiritual insights came about with more frequency. Whenever the thought of "self" or "I" flashed across his mind, it was likely to be accompanied by a sensation of emptiness, of "no I."

"Previously," the Dalai Lama said, "unless I think seriously and continuously at least for a few minutes, it was difficult to get that kind of feeling. Nowadays, as soon as I remember about emptiness, the picture becomes clearly different."

"Is this a stronger realization of emptiness?" I asked.

"Yes," the Dalai Lama said. Then he promptly backtracked: "Emptiness . . . I don't know." I had the feeling he wanted to be very careful about this.

"What's the importance in seeing the intangible in things? What has that got to do with your life?" I asked.

The Dalai Lama spoke to Lhakdor.

"Normally we tend to see things in a solid, tangible way," Lhakdor translated. "Therefore, there is a tendency to grasp at things, to become attached to things. We cling to the idea of a separate self and separate things. We strive for new experiences, new acquisitions. Yet as soon as we possess them, the buzz is gone, and we look for something new. This endless cycle of craving brings suffering.

"In His Holiness' case, this grasping attitude does not arise. This is because the 'self,' wishes, desires, or Rolex watches are perceived ultimately by him as impermanent, changing, elusive. Empty. Like mirages, they are not quite real. There is no way you can truly hang on to them. Therefore, there is no point to covet them. If we acquire an understanding of emptiness, craving, the source of our suffering, is lessened."

The Dalai Lama lapsed into Tibetan once again. Something had tickled his funny bone. He launched into one of his full-body laughing fits, waggling his head from side to side. His face was so crunched up with mirth that his eyes disappeared.

"His Holiness says he's boasting. And he says this is called a fool trying to fool others," Lhakdor said with a big smile.

I looked over the notes I'd jotted down. The interview was veering in a direction I had not expected. A new thought occurred to me, and I asked the Dalai Lama: "Did you ever talk to anyone about your spiritual accomplishment?"

"In the early seventies," he replied, "I told Ling Rinpoche, almost like report, about my understanding of emptiness, then he . . ." He trailed off, turning to speak to Lhakdor in Tibetan.

"Ling Rinpoche commented that very soon His Holiness will become a space yogi," Lhakdor translated. "A space yogi is a practitioner who realizes spacelike emptiness, someone who has achieved substantive enlightenment."

"Did you get into that state?" I asked, throwing caution to the wind.

"I don't know," the Dalai Lama said. I noticed that he seemed to be twiddling his thumbs, but after a second I realized that his hands, resting comfortably on his lap, were rhythmically clicking the beads of an imaginary rosary. He spoke to Lhakdor again.

"All the time he's making progress," Lhakdor translated. "His Holiness is quite sure about one thing. If Ling Rinpoche was still alive today, and His Holiness told him about his spiritual attainment, Ling Rinpoche would definitely be pleased.

"There is a reason why His Holiness is explaining all this to you," Lhakdor said, unprompted. "Normally it is totally improper to talk about these things."

"That's right, that's right. Therefore, whenever I explain some of my experiences about compassion and my understanding of emptiness, I always make clear . . ." the Dalai Lama said. He switched to Tibetan and spoke directly to Lhakdor.

"His Holiness sometimes talks about his spiritual development to inspire people," Lhakdor translated, "but he always concludes by saying: 'I'm not saying I'm bodhisattva; I'm not saying I've realized emptiness.' His Holiness also makes this point: from his own experience, he notices that one can always make progress. Therefore, he would tell his audience: 'In my own case also, even though I am not a bodhisattva, have not cultivated *bodhicitta*—infinite altruism—but I'm like someone who can now see the top of the mountain.' "

The Dalai Lama interjected. "Not reached top, but now I get the feeling—oh, I can get there," he said and pinched his nose.

"You can smell it," I suggested.

The shadows were lengthening on the charming veranda outside the room. The Dalai Lama looked at his watch and said to me, "Now, five more minutes." I had been with him for nearly two hours, but I felt a slight panic coming on. I still had a page and a half of questions to go. As I considered my next question, Lhakdor turned to look at me and said: "There is always some danger talking about things like spiritual development."

"Danger?" I was nonplussed. I was also surprised that Lhakdor had offered up this caution on his own, and in the presence of the Dalai Lama. It was his habit to remain silent unless he was called upon to translate.

"If you say you have realized emptiness, while in actual fact you have not attained that state," Lhakdor explained.

"The danger is this," the Dalai Lama elaborated. "Although I do not have that intention, on the basis of my statement, someone believes I have attained some higher state. If he believes it out of faith, maybe all right. But if he believes it because of my statement, and then if I feel . . ." He paused.

Lhakdor completed the thought for the Dalai Lama. "If His Holiness feels, 'It is OK, it is fine that he gets such an idea,' then there is a risk."

"So there is some selfish motivation now," the Dalai Lama added.

As I had been at other times, I was struck by how unflinchingly the Dalai Lama examines his motivation for every act. It is a conditioned response; it happens every time he opens his mouth or makes a decision.

"Lie, of course, whether layperson or monk, everyone, lying is sin, negative," the Dalai Lama continued, with heightened intensity. "But I'm monk, fully ordained. If I tell others that I have some deep experience of spiritual realization, and knowing I have not that quality, that lie is one major lie. It is cause for disrobing—no longer monk."

"It's not like telling a minor lie; it's a very big, special lie," Lhakdor added.

"Like sexual misconduct, killing human being, stealing. Then this lie," the Dalai Lama said.

"Four major ones," I said.

"Then no longer as monk. Therefore, it's dangerous," the Dalai Lama concluded.

Our interview was at an end. The Dalai Lama walked over and gave me a hug. After he left the room, I started to gather up the things I'd strewn all over the coffee table—notebooks, sheaves of typed questions, photocopies of articles, tape recorder. Lhakdor hung around and helped me cram them into my day pack. We didn't make small talk as we usually did after a session; I felt drained, and he seemed to be as well. As we walked out of the audience room, Lhakdor gently touched my elbow. I turned to look at him. His face seemed soft, a touch vulnerable.

"You know, Victor," he said to me quietly, "I've heard His Holiness touch on these subjects briefly before. But I've never heard him go into such detail, such depth. The monks and lamas in the monasteries wouldn't believe their ears if they heard that interview." His eyes sought out mine. "They'd be so inspired, so moved, they'd go crazy."

14.

White Kites Fluttering

꧁ I liked the hotel room. It was spacious and high-ceilinged, one of a few guest rooms in the Circuit House, a colonial mansion used by Indian officials on government business in Rajgir, the small town near Vultures' Peak. It was the bathroom I didn't care for. There was no hot water, and the toilet was Eastern—a hole in the floor. I have never developed the necessary leg muscles or the flexibility to cope with these contraptions. The room, however, opened onto a large veranda, furnished with a few rattan chairs and low tables. I could easily imagine sitting here at sunset, dressed in white linen, sipping an ice-cold gin and tonic garnished with a wedge of lime. I was staying at the Circuit House courtesy of the Private Office of the Dalai Lama. The room charge was ten rupees a night—twenty U.S. cents—for which the government of India would duly invoice Dharamsala.

I hadn't expected to spend the night here, but there had been a change of plan. For the last couple of weeks, I had accompanied the Dalai Lama on his pilgrimage to some of the most important Buddhist sites of India. After the strenuous walk up Vultures' Peak, the Dalai Lama had decided to go directly to a hotel in Patna, a three-hour drive away. It would break up his long, uncomfortable journey back to Bodhgaya along the notoriously bad roads of Bihar; he'd arrive rested and be better prepared to begin the great Kalachakra ritual before 200,000 pilgrims. I had decided against going with the Dalai Lama to Patna. I couldn't face such a long drive so late in the day.

I shared the hotel room with Dr. Tseten Dorji Sadutshang, one of the Dalai Lama's principal physicians. He joined me as I was getting ready for bed. He is by nature a quiet and reserved man, although he has always been friendly to me. We have a few things in common. Part of his family lives in Vancouver, my hometown, and we both have preteen children. We also enjoy long thoughtful chats about the Dalai Lama.

Before we turned off the lights, Dr. Tseten told me why he was in Rajgir, why he had, on his own initiative, followed the Dalai Lama on his pilgrimage to Vultures' Peak and Nalanda. The roads are bad in these out-of-the-way places, and medical facilities are few and far between. So Dr. Tseten had come along just in case. It wasn't easy to be the Dalai Lama's doctor, he confided. The Tibetan leader tends to get annoyed when his staff fusses over him. He rebels at the idea of having doctors around him when he travels; he believes that doctors should be serving the public rather than hovering at his elbow. Over the years, Dr. Tseten has become reconciled to this, and he's learned to shadow his patient surreptitiously.

By the time I woke up in the morning, Dr. Tseten had already left the room. I took a bracingly cold shower, packed my things, and went out to the terrace. I sat down in a wingback wicker chair, enjoying the cool morning air. A thin wash of mist softened the red earth. A couple of street dogs, dead to the world after a night of adventures, were curled up in tight balls under a tree. All was quiet except for the birds.

Suddenly Dr. Tseten bounded up the stairs, taking the steps two at a time. Without so much as a good morning, he said to me: "OK, the car is here. We have to leave right away. There is no time for breakfast." He grabbed his stuff from the room and ran down the stairs. I followed closely behind.

As we drove out of the Circuit House compound, Dr. Tseten filled me in. He had gotten an early-morning call from Tenzin Taklha, His Holiness' deputy private secretary. The Dalai Lama had suffered from severe abdominal pain on the way to Patna and had spent the night there, in the Maurya Hotel. He was in no condition to continue on to Bodhgaya. After hanging up, Dr. Tseten had called his colleagues—Dr.

Namgyal and Dr. Dawa, specialists in Tibetan medicine who staffed a free clinic for pilgrims in Bodhgaya. They too would head out to Patna immediately.

THE MAURYA, sandwiched between a couple of seedy-looking apartment buildings, was the best hotel in Patna. Its small lobby was crowded with Indian journalists; this would be their command post as they waited for news about the Dalai Lama's condition. A bodyguard took Dr. Tseten upstairs right away. I went to the restaurant for breakfast, then made my way up to the third floor. A phalanx of Tibetan security personnel hung around the corridor. Dr. Tseten and Tenzin Taklha were nowhere to be seen.

The situation looked serious. I could see that the Dalai Lama's bodyguards were concerned; there was none of their usual banter. And all three of the physicians charged with looking after the Dalai Lama had come here to check on his condition. In all the years I have known him, since my first audience in 1972, the Tibetan leader had never been sick except for the occasional flu or upset stomach. The only time he'd been seriously ill was when he contracted hepatitis B in 1967. He had been laid up for a month then, and the exile community had been traumatized.

Late that morning, I went back to Bodhgaya without Dr. Tseten. I was nagged by an uneasy feeling as my driver negotiated his way out of the heavy traffic of Patna.

AFTER THREE DAYS of rest in Patna, the Dalai Lama's condition had not improved. He was flown to the small airport in Gaya by a government helicopter. From there he was driven the short distance to Shechen Monastery in the heart of Bodhgaya. As he got out of the car unsteadily, he was welcomed by Chime-la, the tall, big-boned daughter of the late Dilgo Khyentse Rinpoche, the legendary founder of the monastery. The Dalai Lama grabbed her left arm and leaned on her with all his weight as they shuffled to the entrance. Rabjam Rinpoche, the current abbot, averted his eyes. Tears rolled down his cheeks; he was devastated at how haggard the Dalai Lama looked.

THE EIGHT-YEAR-OLD incarnate lama sat behind a low table draped with intricately patterned brocades. The vividness of the fabrics' colors competed for attention with the profusion of flowers on the table. Yellow marigolds were piled on shallow copper dishes filled with water; bunches of pink gladiola were mixed with pale purple lilacs in a brass vase. An oversize backrest on which embroidered dragons frolicked on surfaces of gold dwarfed the young boy. Yangsi Rinpoche, in his yellow and maroon robes, carried himself like a prince on his throne. Flanked by Rabjam Rinpoche and other high lamas, he sat before a large assembly of Tibetan monks. They were gathered in the courtyard of the Mahabodhi Temple of Bodhgaya to pray for the speedy recovery of the Dalai Lama. The ailing Tibetan leader had been in Bodhgaya for a few days, and there were no signs that he was getting any better.

A Tibetan monk wearing a white surgical mask approached the chubby-faced boy; he was holding a wire cage out in front of him. Inside the cage was a rose-ringed parakeet, a green bird the size of a small parrot. Bending low, the monk presented the cage to Yangsi Rinpoche, who leaned forward and blew on the creature—a benediction for a fellow sentient being. He then reached for the metal ring on top of the cage. The skittish bird suddenly flapped its wings violently and the startled boy withdrew his hand in a hurry. The monk opened the door of the cage. The bird flung itself clumsily against the opening. There was a flash of green, and then it was off. The boy lama, pleased with himself, stole a quick glance at Rabjam Rinpoche. The senior lama had a big grin on his face. His young charge, with a little help, had just performed an act of merit that just might have an effect on the Dalai Lama's health.

A group of elderly Tibetan pilgrims sat some distance away from me. One man was busy working his homemade prayer wheel, a thick wooden rod topped with a skirt of yellow cloth with prayers stenciled on it. He had stuck the rod into the ground and was twirling it in a clockwise direction, the skirt a yellow blur. The man seated next to him was craning his neck, following the trajectory of the freed bird for as long as he could.

*T*HE DALAI LAMA had not left his bedroom on the top floor of Shechen Monastery since he'd arrived from Patna. His doctors and his personal attendant of many years, Paljor-la, were the only ones who had seen him. Tenzin Taklha had taken to wandering vacantly around the monastic grounds with a folderful of documents: daily briefings, communications from the Tibetan cabinet and the Private Office, decisions that required the Dalai Lama's urgent attention. But there were no meetings, no audiences, no teachings with His Holiness.

As he lay sequestered, 200,000 pilgrims poured into the small town where the Buddha had attained enlightenment. All of them were eager for a glimpse of the Dalai Lama and impatient for the great Kalachakra Initiation to begin.

*F*OUR INDIAN COMMANDOS carrying automatic weapons jogged through the gate into the huge Kalachakra compound, their black head scarves streaming behind them. The white Ambassador carrying the Dalai Lama slowly followed. The car came to a stop, and the Tibetan leader stepped out. I had not seen him for ten days, and I was shocked. Instead of a vigorous man who could pass for someone in his mid-fifties, he now looked every inch sixty-seven years old.

His shoulders more hunched than usual, the Dalai Lama waddled along the yellow carpet—a red carpet wrapped in yellow cotton—that had been laid out for him. As he arrived at a receiving line of monks and Tibetan officials, all holding bunches of incense, he scraped an index finger down his wan right cheek and said something to the nearest monk. I guessed he was asking if he had gotten thinner. There was no question that he had lost weight. The hollows in his cheeks were more pronounced; his eyes were sunken. As he walked past me, his face crinkled into a tentative smile. But I was acutely aware that he didn't have the energy to raise his hand in greeting, as was his custom.

The Dalai Lama shuffled through the small Kalachakra chapel housing the sand mandala and out onto a large stage. Four hundred of the most senior monks from all four schools of Tibetan Buddhism were waiting patiently for his arrival. There had been an announcement two days earlier that the Dalai Lama would make a brief appearance at the Kalachakra grounds—his first public event since he'd fallen ill. Excitement had rippled through Bodhgaya and beyond. Below the stage a sizable contingent of journalists and TV crews jockeyed for a view of the ailing Tibetan leader.

Little Yangsi Rinpoche, together with half a dozen incarnate lamas, sat in the front row. The Dalai Lama walked up to the boy and patted his head. As His Holiness started to climb the wooden steps leading to his throne, several pairs of hands grabbed his arms to steady him. A thickset monk high-stepped to the top of the stairs for better leverage and physically pulled the weakened Dalai Lama up. The Tibetan leader stood a touch unsteadily on the thick cushion. Palms pressed together in front of his chest, he bowed solemnly to the giant crowd gathered before him. Hundreds of thousands of pilgrims from the entire arc of the Himalayas and the Indian subcontinent had squeezed into the makeshift compound, along with 2,000 Westerners from fifty countries.

After he sat down, the Dalai Lama fumbled inside his robes and took out a piece of paper. That was unusual. He had always spoken extemporaneously. I looked away to scan the crowd below. Out of the corner of my eye, I saw something that looked like a white, elongated bird floating through the air above the large crowd of monks sitting below. One monk, without moving from his lotus position, had reached inside his satchel and taken out a khata—a white ceremonial scarf. He crumpled it into a ball and threw it out over the crowd. It sailed through the air gracefully, powered by a gust. A monk with a long goatee caught it in midstream, then hurled it farther. In no time, as if by some unseen cue, hundreds of soft silk cloths streaked across the air like so many silk kites, forming a shimmering, ever-changing web of white above a sea of red. Unable to get near the stage to physically present the scarves to the ailing Tibetan leader, the monks and pilgrims were doing the next best thing.

The Dalai Lama sat hunched on his throne, taking in the scene. He took a deep breath, cleared his throat, and swallowed. He inhaled with effort a couple of times. I got the sense that it was an emotional moment for him, that he was deeply touched by the outpouring of concern from so many people. I would always remember those few seconds. The grounds were packed, but not a cough punctuated the silence.

The Dalai Lama started to speak in Tibetan. His deep baritone was still there, but some of its splendor was missing. The illness had robbed him of much of his vitality. His translator, Lhakdor, sat lotus-fashion on one corner of the stage, a small transmitter before him. As the Dalai Lama began to talk to the crowd, Lhakdor spoke softly into his microphone in English. His words would be picked up by the Westerners with FM radios.

"During the last few days, I have been quite sick," Lhakdor translated. "Before that, although I had been healthy, many people had already suggested that I take more rest and not work as hard. I didn't pay much attention to them. So I was careless and a little stubborn." The Dalai Lama told the crowd about his pilgrimage to the Vultures' Peak and his exhausting climb to the top. He talked about the terrible pain he experienced during the drive to Patna.

"I think I'm cured now, but I'm still very tired," he continued. "I don't think I will be able to give the preliminary teachings." I heard some sniffles through my headphones. I looked over at Lhakdor. His head was bowed, and I could see that his face was flushed. "As for the Kalachakra Initiation, it could be shortened to some extent. But its preparation takes at least five to six hours every day—even if I do it quickly. I don't think my present state of health would permit this." There were more sniffles. Lhakdor stopped speaking entirely for a moment as he cleared his throat. "If I force myself to perform these preparations, this would be stubborn. So, for the sake of maintaining my health, to be able to work for the benefit of others over the long term, I have decided to postpone the Kalachakra until next year." On the stage, many of the high lamas and abbots were weeping openly.

"Those of you who have come from far away, do not feel sad that you have not received the Kalachakra Initiation," Lhakdor translated. "You have come to this holy place with determination and the right motivation. You will accumulate merit with every step you take, every action you perform. The main source of blessing is not me. Not the Dalai Lama. It is the holy image of the Buddha, and the sacred ground visited by so many of the greatest spiritual masters. So do not think that you have come here for nothing.

"Normally you cannot view the mandala until after the initiations. However, since I am unable to confer them, this is a slight problem. But you have come to this holy place with great devotion, so I think it will be useful for you to see the mandala."

The Dalai Lama paused to collect his thoughts.

"Right now, funnily enough, my body seems to be improving as I speak to you. If my health does not deteriorate, I'll try to give some teachings for two days. And on the fifteenth day of the Tibetan month, I'll come back here for the last event of the Kalachakra—the long-life empowerment."

ORE TIBETANS continued to arrive in Bodhgaya as the day progressed. That night, the Mahabodhi Temple appeared to be on fire. Its myriad votive stupas and towers with intricate stone carvings were lit by half a million candles, each one an offering for the speedy recovery of the Dalai Lama. Tens of thousands of pilgrims shuffled clockwise in ritual circumambulation. From a distance, the circular precinct looked like a gigantic space station bathed in an otherworldly glow.

I went back to the Kalachakra chapel the following day. The monks from the Dalai Lama's monastery were chanting prayers. A few of their colleagues were working on the colorful and very complex sand mandala, adding one painstaking grain of sand at a time. Everything in the mandala, laid out meticulously on a two-meter-square wooden platform, was a symbolic representation of some aspect of the Kalachakra deity and the deity's universe. At one point I noticed that they had become agitated, whispering among themselves. They had made a small mistake: a tiny figure was inscribed in the wrong location. After making sure no one was watching, a monk surreptitiously sucked the offending grains out through a metal tube. I had seen several sand mandalas being constructed, but this was the first time I had ever seen a flaw. Without the presence of the Dalai Lama, there was a palpable sense of lethargy in the air.

I noticed a tiny mike affixed to the woodwork just above

a window, its wire snaking through a crack to the outside. A monk told me that the wire was hooked up to an FM transmitter that fed a loudspeaker in the Dalai Lama's bedroom. Even in his weakened state, the Dalai Lama wanted to contribute. If he couldn't participate in person, he would make sure he was there in spirit. He wanted to tune in to the monks' prayers, and silently add his—from afar. This collective energy, a paean to world peace, would be released when the mandala was ritually destroyed and its sand emptied into a water source. Until then, the Dalai Lama would compel himself to stay engaged, to follow the meticulous preparations from his sickbed. Picturing him there, willing himself to remain conscious to the chants, I was once again touched by his humanity.

15.

A Couple of Unsigned Photographs

The lead Korean dancer was in a trance. Her eyes were closed, a crazed smile frozen on her face. She whipped her head back and forth in a frenzy, jerking violently in place to a staccato beat drummed out by her fellow dancers. There were six of them, all wearing pink silk tunics and white baggy trousers. A few had hats piled extravagantly high with pink and yellow pompoms. The dancers were part of a sizable contingent of Korean Buddhists in Bodhgaya for the Kalachakra Initiations. After the morning teachings by a Tibetan lama, a small group of them had decided to provide the monks with some diversion, to take their minds away from the uncertainty about the Dalai Lama's condition.

An old Tibetan woman appeared from nowhere. All of a sudden, she was right in the midst of the dancing Koreans.

She began to sashay back and forth languidly. Once she got into the rhythm, she twisted and pirouetted energetically, flinging her arms around with abandon. She pulled out a long blue scarf, which she whipped around and around over her head, a perfect complement to her flowing Tibetan dress.

The monks were enchanted. This frail and grandmotherly Tibetan, her white hair tied up in a bun, was matching the much younger Koreans beat for beat. They egged her on with shouts and catcalls. A novice monk, about six years of age, climbed onto the shoulders of an older monk to get a better look. A burly Indian policeman stood and stared, forgetting for the moment his job of crowd control. The old woman, a serene smile on her face, paid no attention to the people around her.

An elderly Western woman, grinning hugely and shaking her head in disbelief, walked up to one of the monks. As she caught his attention, she gave him a thumbs-up, then gyrated her arms and shoulders to mimic the dance of the old Tibetan woman. The monk smiled good-naturedly, patted her on the shoulder, and stuck up his own thumb.

After the performance, I went back to my hotel. I sat down in the lobby and read the day's *Times of India*. The Karmapa had checked into the hotel a couple of days earlier, and there were many people hanging around the lobby, hoping to get a glimpse of the seventeen-year-old supreme head of Karma Kagyud sect. Years earlier, the teenager had ditched his Chinese minders in his Tibet monastery, and crossed the

Himalayas on horseback at night, in order to be with the Dalai Lama.

Alan King, a Canadian who has photographed seven Kalachakras over the past decade, slid in beside me. He leaned in close and said in a low voice: "Victor, I don't like the look of this. Tenzin Taklha finally took my two photos to the Dalai Lama this morning. Half an hour ago, he gave them back to me. Unsigned." King was mounting an exhibition of Kalachakra photos in Graz, Austria, and he needed autographs from the Dalai Lama. Talkha had been carrying the photos in his briefcase for days.

"Tenzin didn't get in to see the Dalai Lama?" I asked.

"No. He saw the Dalai Lama and he presented the photos. But he was too weak to sign them."

I had been feeling uneasy about the Dalai Lama for a couple of days. When he'd appeared at the Kalachakra grounds, he had distinctly said he'd give two days of teachings if he recovered enough of his strength. That hadn't happened. Several top lamas had taught in his stead. The final day of the Kalachakra, when the huge crowd would dedicate long-life prayers to the Dalai Lama, was just around the corner. The Dalai Lama had promised he would attend, but so far there had been no official confirmation.

It was thirty years since I'd first met the Dalai Lama. In recent years, we'd flown together, broke bread together, and spent time in his residence in the wee hours of the morning. As we worked on our book, he shared his insights about forgiveness, compassion, and emptiness. Little by little, he had grown on me. By now I saw him as a kind of father figure.

Most important, I knew in my heart that he cared for me. There was the time he had sent me a chair to sit on in a teaching, because he sensed that my legs were not made for sitting lotus-style on the floor. I knew he encouraged Tenzin Geyche to look out for me, to take me out for dinner from time to time so that I wouldn't feel neglected. I was very moved by this knowledge. The fact that the Dalai Lama also has deep connections to so many other people in his orbit, many of them when he met them for the first time, didn't make much of a difference. I didn't begrudge their good fortune. It was enough for me to experience his profound warmth once in a while.

I had been devastated to see him so weakened at the Kalachakra grounds. In a span of ten days, he had aged ten years. And now Alan King was telling me that the Dalai Lama was too weak to pick up a pen.

I left the Mahayana Hotel and walked the short distance to the Mahabodhi Temple. Walking clockwise around the central tower, I began my ritual circumambulation, jostled and pushed along by a large crowd of pilgrims. I stopped at a small open area on the south side of the complex. There, thousands upon thousands of candles and butter lamps burned on stone altars and any other available surface. I bought a small package of candles from the caretaker. I lit one with a tinder, melted the wax at the bottom, then stuck it onto a stone ledge. As I did, I offered a silent prayer for the Dalai Lama. Then I lit the rest of the candles.

After completing the pilgrims' circuit, I headed back to the hotel. Just before I got there, I ran into Tenzin Taklha, hurrying in the opposite direction. I was glad to see him; I wanted the latest update about the Dalai Lama's condition.

Tenzin slowed down but didn't stop. "I can't talk now," he said tersely. "I have just been on the phone with the prime minister. We're evacuating the Dalai Lama first thing tomorrow morning."

In a daze, I walked into the hotel lobby. It was still full of people waiting for the Karmapa to emerge. A small group of Westerners sat on couches near the back. A tall American was showing the others stunning black-and-white pictures of eastern Tibet on a laptop. Someone cracked a joke, and everyone laughed. Werner Herzog, the legendary filmmaker from Germany, passed through with his film crew and his willowy young wife. He had come here to make a documentary of the Kalachakra.

I went back into my room, closed the curtains, and lay down. I could hear the churning of the large crowd out on the streets—pilgrims heading to the temple, pilgrims leaving the temple to go back to their lodgings. I was expecting Senge Rabten, the Dalai Lama's chief bodyguard. Every day around this time he came to my room to use the shower, since there was no hot water at Shechen Monastery. But Rabten never did show up that day.

THE WISDOM OF FORGIVENESS

*I*T WAS EARLY MORNING in Bodhgaya. I had made sure to arrive at Shechen Monastery well ahead of the Dalai Lama's scheduled departure time. The news that he was being evacuated to a private hospital in Bombay had spread, and the street leading to the monastery was completely clogged. There was anxiety in the air. No one knew how sick the Dalai Lama really was; there was little hard news but plenty of rumor. The fact that he'd be hospitalized, for the first time in over three decades, sent shock waves throughout the Tibetan community.

Scores of policemen and soldiers were busy trying to keep the huge horde away from the entrance. As I walked into the monastery, I was surprised to see the queen of Bhutan, unobtrusive in her striped Bhutanese dress, standing forlorn among the crowd. A couple of policemen, obviously unaware of who she was, unceremoniously shoved her to the back.

The courtyard outside the temple was also crowded. The chief magistrate of the town of Gaya was conferring with several of his senior police officers. Off by themselves in a small group were the crack Indian commandos, intimidating and handsome in their all-black outfits. Less exalted soldiers, wearing khakis and blue berets, stood around in knots. Lhakdor was there as well, looking out of place in his maroon robes.

Flashing my Inner Circle pass, I walked into the cramped lobby of the monastery. A dozen of the most eminent lamas of Tibetan Buddhism had gathered on couches in the small sitting area. A trio of orange-robed Sri Lankan monks, administrators of the Mahabodhi temple, sat among them. Trulshik Rinpoche, the last living tutor of the Dalai Lama, came down the stairs. The frail and gentle monk had no doubt been bidding farewell to the Dalai Lama.

I stood to one side of the lobby and waited.

Before long, I saw the Dalai Lama slowly descending the stairs. His faithful attendant of many years, Paljor-la, held him up by his left armpit. Senge Rabten had his hands in a vice grip around the Dalai Lama's right elbow. The Dalai Lama looked haggard, but no more so than when I'd last seen him. However, he apparently had continued to lose weight.

When the Tibetan leader reached the lobby, he went up to the waiting lamas. As was his habit, he kidded around and teased them. He rubbed the head of one and poked someone else in the chest. Even in his weakened state, he still wanted to make them feel good, to lighten their grief. He knew that they were traumatized by his condition.

As he shuffled toward the entrance, the Dalai Lama caught sight of me, half hidden behind some security guards. For a couple of heartbeats, he paused and looked at me steadily. He didn't smile; his eyes simply locked onto mine. I found myself going red, my jaw muscles clenched. The Dalai Lama came forward and embraced me gently. Tears streamed down my face, wetting the fabric of his robes, as I held on to him. He finally pulled away, looked into my teary eyes once more, and walked out into the courtyard.

16.

All the Selfish Buddhas

⟋⟍ Lhakdor sat stiffly on the edge of the couch. The monk-translator was unaccustomedly quiet. It was 4:30 in the morning; maybe it was too early for him. Drolma, the Dalai Lama's German shepherd, lay curled up next to him. She was oblivious to our intrusion into her living area; her stainless-steel food and water bowls were on the floor next to the couch.

It was late March 2002, two and a half months after the Dalai Lama had gotten seriously ill in Bodhgaya. Lhakdor and I were in the ground-floor sitting room of the Dalai Lama's private quarters in Dharamsala. We were about to have a rendezvous with the Tibetan leader. For the first time since his sickness, he was strong enough to receive visitors. And for the second time in three years, I had been given the rare privilege of accompanying the Dalai Lama on his morning walk. I would see for myself whether he had truly recovered.

The sitting room's rattan furniture and area carpets were dowdy and a bit worse for wear. An oil portrait of the Dalai Lama, painted years ago by the looks of it, hung on one wall. A painting of an endless knot floating in a new-age blue ether propped against the legs of a table. It was obvious that the room was seldom used. The Dalai Lama had few reasons to come down here. Everything he needed—his meditation room, his study, his dining room—was on the second floor. And he almost always preferred to meet visitors in the audience hall complex farther down the hill in the residential compound.

One thing that struck me about the sitting room was its bunker-like feel. The building was clearly designed to be earthquake-resistant, perhaps even earthquake-proof. Massive concrete beams girded this bottom floor. The room's low ceiling accentuated its claustrophobic feel.

At precisely 4:40 A.M., a Tibetan bodyguard came in to tell us that the Dalai Lama was on his way downstairs. We left the room and hurried outside. The pleasantly cool night air was heavy with the scent of exotic flowers; nearly all of the available space in the entrance courtyard was crammed with potted plants, masses of purple and dark blue blossoms set off by taller reds in the back. The entire two-story residence was lit up like a ship on high seas, bathing the surrounding grounds with light. Half a dozen Tibetan bodyguards hung around the entrance. While everyone else in Dharamsala slept, this secluded enclave was alive with subdued, purposeful activity.

The Dalai Lama slowly walked down the heavily reinforced external stairs. He was wearing his monk's robes but had left the outer shawl behind; his shoulders and arms were bare. After nodding to Lhakdor, he leaned in close to peer at me, straightened up, boomed a hearty "Ni hao?"—his standard greeting for me in Chinese—and walked off at a brisk pace. It had been more than two months since I'd last seen him. At the time, he had been shuffling laboriously out of Shechen Monastery in Bodhgaya en route to the small Gaya airport. A helicopter had been on standby to take him to one of the best hospitals in India. On this early spring morning, however, he looked alert and vital, if a touch gaunt. There seemed no doubt that he had recovered from his debilitating illness. Two Indian officers in khakis and windbreakers appeared from nowhere and took off after him. The Tibetan bodyguards, Lhakdor, and I brought up the rear.

We soon left the eerie glow cast by the residence behind. Walking along a wide concrete path, we passed a long, narrow greenhouse. Then we headed up into a dark, heavily wooded area. A lone Indian sentry, wearing a short overcoat against the cold, stood at attention next to a concrete shelter, his rifle smartly cradled against his side. The Dalai Lama walked up to him, playfully tugged at his rifle, and said good morning. The soldier seemed used to this routine. He kept his eyes fixed at a level spot in front of him and said crisply, "Good morning, sir."

We skirted the bottom of a small hill topped with prayer flags and a white stupa. The path narrowed as we approached the audience hall complex. It was pitch dark in this area. A bodyguard had gone on ahead and turned on his powerful flashlight, illuminating the path and the bougainvillea-clad veranda. The Dalai Lama rounded a circular driveway and headed uphill to his private chapel. From the other side of the building, a steep path descending through thick woods led back down to the residence. The Dalai Lama slowed to a crawl during the last section, mincing his steps as he negotiated the tricky incline in the dim light. Then we were back where we had started. I was pleasantly surprised when the Dalai Lama turned around to begin another circuit. The first time I had accompanied him on one of these early-morning jaunts, he had walked to a point just beyond the greenhouse and then turned back—covering in total a distance not much greater than the width of a football field. In the two years since then, I have often nagged him about the importance of exercise, and I was gratified that he had taken it seriously. On that morning, the Dalai Lama completed three circuits in all. At the end of his regime, he said good-bye to us and went back upstairs to take a shower and have breakfast. The walk had taken nearly half an hour, and I was sweating in spite of the cool mountain air.

Even from the little I had seen of the Dalai Lama in the dim, predawn light, I could tell he had lost weight. Not a surprise, given that he had been bedridden for most of January and February. In a few hours, I was scheduled to begin an-

other series of interviews with him. I was keen to quiz him
about his illness.

WHEN I WALKED into the audience hall that afternoon, I was pleasantly surprised to see Ngari Rinpoche there with Lhakdor. The Tibetan leader's youngest
brother didn't sit in on all my interviews, but the odd times he
did, usually at the request of His Holiness, his highly developed sense of humor helped take the edge off my nervousness.
The Dalai Lama came into the room shortly afterward, right
on time as usual. He sat down in his armchair and looked at
me expectantly.

"How are you feeling now?" I began.

"OK. Only problem, gas," he replied.

"Distension of the abdomen, lots of gas," Ngari Rinpoche
elaborated.

"Gas increase, then sometimes a little sore. But walk, no
problem," the Dalai Lama said. I noticed he was sitting on the
edge of his armchair rather than leaning back against it as he
usually did. And his English was noticeably more choppy.

I was particularly interested to know what had happened
to the Dalai Lama after our pilgrimage to the ruins of Nalanda
and to Vultures' Peak. He told me that he had developed
acute stomach pain well before the motorcade reached Patna.
The pain was so severe that he'd curled up into a tight ball.
Trying to get comfortable, he'd shifted positions, leaning
against the car door, facing first one way and then another.

Finally he gave up and settled on his left side, slumping his head and shoulder against the hand rest. Every bump of the road sent an excruciating jolt through his body. His eyes were closed and he was sweating profusely, in spite of the air-conditioning being turned up high.

Before the interview with the Dalai Lama, I had spoken to the Indian liaison officer charged with coordinating security arrangements. I wanted to know about the car ride from Na-landa to Patna. The officer had accompanied the Dalai Lama during his many trips in India. But he had never seen him in such a state of agony. Mild diarrhea or a cold, yes. But never like this. The Dalai Lama was hunched up like a sick dog, and Patna was still an hour away. The officer radioed the lead po-lice escort of the convoy, telling him about the problem. The motorcade sped up, sirens blaring and lights flashing. Cars and lorries pulled to the side of the road to allow the dozen-odd cars to pass. The increased speed smoothed out some of the potholes, and that seemed to make the Dalai Lama feel slightly better.

On the outskirts of Patna, however, the convoy had slowed to a crawl. The road was choked with early-evening traffic, and the din was horrendous; every driver, or so it seemed to the Dalai Lama, was leaning on his horn. Even with the police escort, there was no way for the convoy to go any faster. It was wedged tightly among several diesel-belching buses and darting three-wheelers. Because of the frequent stops and starts, the Dalai Lama started to feel sick to his stomach. He managed to prop himself up to a sitting position, and he found that his nausea eased when he could look out the window.

That was when he saw an old man and a young boy by the side of the road.

"I was very painful; very, very painful," the Dalai Lama described the scene to me in the audience hall. Ngari Rinpoche hung on to his every word; he had not heard these details before. "Then all this liquid . . . water . . . sweat. This time I noticed: water from eyes, much connected with emotion. Water from body, much connected with physical pain. So when very serious physical pain comes, no water from eyes, only from body. What's the difference, what's the connection, I don't know. Then I saw one old person with long, untrimmed hair." The Dalai Lama passed his right hand over the crown of his head. Spreading his thumb and little finger wide, he gave me an idea of how long the old man's hair had been. "And beard. Completely disheveled. Wearing clothes soaked with dust and filth." He grimaced as he recalled the disturbing image.

"Then so many poor children. No education, living by the side of the road. I noticed one this size." The Dalai Lama extended his arm to indicate a height of three to four feet; he then reached down to touch his shins with both hands. "Suffering from polio, both his legs having clamps. And he was using crutches. So while I had this physical pain, in my eyes there was only the image of these poor people. No one cared for them while I was getting good care."

The Dalai Lama closed his eyes and fell silent. After a few

moments, he continued. "Although I felt physical pain, mentally no anxiety, quite peaceful. Just felt a little inconvenience. Why that peaceful feeling? I myself get physical pain, but mentally constantly feeling about these other people who have no care. Therefore not much worry about my own pain. Concern for others seems to help lessen my own pain. The experience of generating compassion is something very beneficial to oneself, not necessarily beneficial to others. I reflected on the terrible condition of the old man, the boy with polio. My sense of concern reduced the feeling of my own physical pain. So, very good."

"Is this what you have in mind," I asked the Dalai Lama, "when you say in teachings that the buddhas and bodhisattvas of the world are the most selfish beings of all, that by cultivating altruism they actually achieve ultimate happiness for themselves?"

"Yes. That's wise selfish," he replied. "Helping others not means we do this at our own expense. Not like this. Buddhas and bodhisattvas, these people very wise. All their lives they only want one thing: to achieve ultimate happiness. How to do this? By cultivating compassion, by cultivating altruism. When they care for others, they themselves are the first to benefit—they are first to get maximum happiness. They know best way to lead happy life is help others. That's real wisdom. They don't think: 'Oh, I'm most important, other people not so important.' Not that way. Intentionally they consider others' well-being to be the most important. And, in reality, this action returns maximum benefit to them."

A thought occurred to the Dalai Lama. He turned to Ngari Rinpoche and said in English, "I think cook . . ." He trailed off into Tibetan. His youngest brother translated: "A cook who cooks for others, even though he doesn't have the intention of cooking for himself, is always well fed."

"Many cooks very fat, I noticed," the Dalai Lama added. He and his brother had a good laugh over this.

"So did your pain actually go away when you saw those poor people in Patna?" I wanted to know.

"No, I don't think," the Dalai Lama said. "But these mental pictures of what I saw, the poverty and helplessness, they were very sharp. Even when I lay in my Patna hotel bed, I was in pain, but all I saw was those two. Hungry, thirsty. Over and over in my mind, I asked: 'What a pity! What can we do, what can we do?' So the intensity of my pain reduced. Something like being overwhelmed by strong concern."

17.

The Coldness of Blueberries

⬯ Ever since I left Bodhgaya, I had been obsessed with a nagging question: how could the Dalai Lama's stomach pains escalate into a full-blown crisis, precipitating his evacuation to a specialist hospital in Bombay? I wanted to explore the causes of his illness with the Dalai Lama.

"Did you feel bad when you walked up the steep hill to Vultures' Peak?" I asked him in his audience room. Ngari Rinpoche moved his straight-backed chair a little closer to his brother. He hadn't gone to Vultures' Peak with us, and he was interested to know what had transpired before the onset of the Dalai Lama's pain.

"No," the Dalai Lama replied. "I didn't feel bad that morning. Nothing. Very fresh. But then inside, already some causes and conditions."

"Did you eat something bad at the Japanese hotel in Rajgir?"

"I don't think."

"But you had diarrhea after having lunch at the hotel?"

"Dysentery."

"I heard from Dr. Tseten there were amoebas in your stomach. They must have come from bad food or bad water."

"I don't know," the Dalai Lama replied. "How long the amoebas in my stomach I don't know. Not necessary come that very day. . . . There are many causes. One, the immediate cause, is carelessness."

"Carelessness?"

"Carelessness because generally my body OK, then I thought . . ." The Dalai Lama looked over to Lhakdor and switched to Tibetan.

"His Holiness felt he was very healthy, so he kept pushing himself, doing too much, traveling too much," Lhakdor translated.

"Less caution," the Dalai Lama explained.

People who work closely with the Dalai Lama would agree with this sentiment wholeheartedly. He keeps a punishing schedule, especially when he is on the road. I have traveled with him enough times to know this for myself. I'm ten years younger. But his energy and stamina put me to shame. Keeping up with him is definitely not a walk in the park.

"Then morning walk up Vultures' Peak, lots of sweat," the Dalai Lama continued. "On top of mountain, little bit cold.

Go back down, sweating again, then lunchtime, took off clothes. After lunch, took fresh lemon and water—usually no problem, but that day, because something already disturbed, then that became one of the factors.

"A more substantial cause. Before I went on pilgrimage to Vultures' Peak and Nalanda, I first went to South India to give teachings. While I was there, I started taking one Tibetan medicine, for liver and for eyes. It is a cold medicine—it gives coldness to the body. Some thirty years ago, I took that same medicine for liver problem, and immediately little pain started here in my stomach. I discontinued and took medicine to generate heat instead. Pain disappear completely. Now this time, exactly same place. So, too much cold."

Too much cold. That was what my mother used to tell me whenever I was sick. It didn't matter much what my symptoms were. The problem was always "cold vapors." She'd drag me clear across Hong Kong island by tram to outlying West Point, where we'd walk up a steep, narrow lane paved with uneven stone steps, to an herbalist's shop. The place was dimly lit, and most of its available wall space was lined with bank upon bank of small rosewood drawers, all filled with herbs. The herbalist would take my pulse, peer at my tongue, write up a prescription with brush and ink, and weigh out herbs from the drawers. Back at our flat, my mother would boil and reduce the herbs for a couple of hours, until the resultant broth was the blackest shade of black. The medicine, though bitter, was not entirely unpleasant. I had to drink the whole thing down in one go while it was piping hot. Usually I got better quite soon after—perhaps in spite of the medicine, I liked to think.

"Like Chinese medicine, like Indian Ayurvedic medicine, Tibetan medicine usually divided into hot and cold," the Dalai Lama elaborated. "Most illnesses of lower body are connected with too much cold. Liver problems, headaches mean too much heat. So for three weeks in south India, every morning I took that medicine, which increased coldness in my body. Little pain occasionally already started. Then during the pilgrimage, immediate causes happened; then something burst.

"Now another factor," he continued. "Last May when I was in America, my digestion system very good, excellent. So during breakfast I took a lot of cold milk. Then in Salt Lake City, one lady, she told me blueberries very good for eyes. She told me American Air Force pilots usually eat lots of blueberry jam. So I took some blueberries, quite tasty. Then day by day, increased. That affected digestion system to some extent—too much cold."

The Dalai Lama spoke briefly to Lhakdor. "It seems that was how the whole thing started," Lhakdor translated, "because of the cold of the blueberries."

So, IT WAS the coldness of the blueberries that triggered the crisis. It was not quite the answer I'd expected. But then I'd reconciled myself to the fact that the Dalai Lama is not like you and me. He has a significantly different way

THE COLDNESS OF BLUEBERRIES

of looking at the world around him. There were still a few things about the illness that I wanted to know.

"What happened when you were in Bodhgaya," I asked the Dalai Lama, "after you came back from Patna?"

"For four, five days in Shechen, not much improvement. Therefore I thought: if Kalachakra started, if once started then failed, then worse. Therefore it's better to cancel, postpone. Then I decided. At beginning, still hope to give three days of teachings. But couldn't do it. Then one morning Dr. Tseten noticed this side of body swollen," the Dalai Lama said, patting the left side of his abdomen.

"He suggested that His Holiness go to the hospital that very day," Lhakdor said.

"That's why you had to cancel the long-life prayers on the last day of the Kalachakra?" I asked.

"Yes," the Dalai Lama said. "That very day, impossible to arrange travels. Then tried to find out whether possible to leave for the Bombay hospital the next day. Some contact with Delhi. State government agreed to provide one helicopter; the central government provided one special flight from Patna to Bombay directly. In Bombay, from airport direct to hospital."

"When His Holiness walked into the hospital," Ngari Rinpoche said to me, unprompted, "the first thing he saw was the IV bottle and the big needle waiting for him. He felt uncomfortable. He was a little scared." Although Ngari Rinpoche was there mainly to help Lhakdor with the translation, I could always trust him to come up with some interesting tidbits.

"But there was no choice, so I had to take the IV," the Dalai Lama said, grimacing slightly at the memory.

"What tests did they do in the hospital?" I asked.

"They checked everything. The stomach, intestine, of course. But also the heart, liver, blood. Nothing wrong. No cancer."

"But what caused the swelling?" I asked.

"They're unable to trace it. Although one specialist told me . . ." The Dalai Lama trailed off again into Tibetan.

"After he examined His Holiness," Ngari Rinpoche translated, "the specialist said things were completely OK, no sign of cancer. Then he mentioned: this was serious illness. It could have killed him. There was a tiny perforation of the intestine. And if it was bigger, it could have killed him."

I glanced at the Dalai Lama, who had the ghost of a smile on his face. It was as if he was secretly amused that he could have died.

A couple of monks came into the audience room, bringing trays. One monk carefully set a lidded cup of hot water next to the Dalai Lama. Another placed a tray with a jar of instant Nescafé, some tea bags, and a Thermos of hot water on the low table next to me. As silently as they had come, they left the room. Ngari Rinpoche got up from his chair, walked over, and whispered into my ear, "Would you like coffee or tea?"

I kept my eyes on the Dalai Lama. "Coffee, please." I was vaguely aware of Rinpoche putting a heaping teaspoon of Nescafé into a cup and then filling it with hot water. He leaned close to me and whispered into my ear again, "Milk? Sugar?"

"Uh, sure, thank you," I replied automatically. As I flipped through my pages of typed questions, a touch of panic gripped me: I had lost the place of my last question, and I had no idea what I was supposed to ask the Dalai Lama next. Coffee was always enormously welcome: midway through a two-hour-plus interview, my energies tended to flag. But sometimes the interruption could knock me off my tenuous focus.

Then I remembered something Dr. Tseten had mentioned to me in a conversation.

"Dr. Tseten told me that the Indian doctors in Bombay said your heart is like that of a twenty-year-old's," I said to the Dalai Lama.

"Yes, that's right," he replied. "After doing the ECG tests, the Bombay doctors informed me. Actually, the Patna doctor who examined me said exactly the same thing."

"What do you think is the reason for this?" I asked as I gulped down my instant coffee greedily.

"I think peace of mind," the Dalai Lama said without hesitation.

"Your heart is like a twenty-year-old's because you have peace of mind?"

"Yes." The Dalai Lama was emphatic. "Otherwise, there is nothing special about me. I don't do any special exercises."

A sixty-seven-year-old man with the heart of a twenty-year-old. The Dalai Lama has no doubt that the mind has the power to heal the body. To him, the mind and the body belong to an inseparable continuum. When something happens to one, the other is affected—the interdependence of all things has been the Dalai Lama's mantra for half a century. Nowadays, even mainstream doctors and researchers are coming to the same conclusion. A disorder in the kidney can have grave consequences for the brain. And depression is now considered a major risk factor for heart disease—it may well be as bad as high cholesterol. After all, body and mind share the same building blocks—blood, nerves, hormones, antibodies.

This was how the Dalai Lama puts it: "Training of the mind, this means strengthening those positive emotions such as forgiveness and compassion, such as dedication to others' welfare. Negative emotions like hatred, jealousy, these are what you call enemies. These negative emotions, through training, we can minimize. This mind training, according to some scientists, is very much relevant to our health.

"Take forgiveness. Two levels here. One level: forgiveness means you shouldn't develop feelings of revenge. Because revenge harms the other person, therefore it is a form of violence. With violence, there is usually counterviolence. This generates even more violence—the problem never goes away. So that is one level. Another level: forgiveness means you should try not to develop feelings of anger toward your enemy. Anger doesn't solve the problem. Anger only brings uncomfortable feelings to yourself. Anger destroys your own peace of mind. Your happy mood never comes, not while anger remains. I think that's the main reason why we should forgive. With calm mind, more peaceful mind, more healthy body. An agitated mind spoils our health, very harmful for body. This is my feeling."

I asked the Dalai Lama if he thought something positive had come about because of his illness. Tibetans around the world had been extremely worried about him. While he lay in his sickbed in Shechen Monastery, a hundred thousand pilgrims stayed out all night in the open air, offering prayers for the Dalai Lama amid decidedly wintry conditions.

The Dalai Lama chose to reply in Tibetan, letting Lhakdor translate: "His Holiness says that the episode was a good activating force for performing good deeds, for pursuing spiritual activities."

I didn't quite understand.

"If everything is normal," the Dalai Lama explained, "then although we pray lots, the prayers may not be very serious. But because I was sick, every prayer was serious. We all took our prayers seriously. So through that way, some positive results."

"The sickness was a catalyst for us to be more spiritual," Ngari Rinpoche summed up.

To the Dalai Lama, suffering and adversity are the necessary conditions for developing patience and tolerance. These qualities are vital if we want to reduce negative emotions like hatred or anger. When things go well, we have less need to be patient and forgiving. It's only when we come across problems, when we suffer, that we truly learn these virtues. Once we internalize them, compassion flows naturally.

W ERE YOU SAD when I depart?" the Dalai Lama asked me unexpectedly.

"I was sad, yes," I replied.

"Did you think His Holiness will not make it?" Ngari Rinpoche was curious.

"No, no. I had some faith. I somehow knew he'd be all right," I replied. "I was sad because he seemed so weak, so vulnerable. I'd never seen him looking so frail before. It shocked me, just as it shocked so many people. And another thing. He gave me a hug before he left Shechen Monastery. I was very touched by that. Even though he was in pain and could hardly stand up, he still wanted to comfort me, to cheer me up. As sick as he was, he still managed to keep an eye out for me. As he always does, he put the welfare of others before his own."

18.

Meditating to the Beeb

I stood next to the Dalai Lama on his rooftop. The view of the Outer Himalayas from here was panoramic. I could make out the three mist-softened ridges cascading gently from the 4,350-meter Indrahar Pass to the broad, verdant Kangra Valley floor below. Farther away in the distance, and considerably higher, was the snow-tinged ridgeline of the Dhauladhar range. On the flank of the near ridge, I spotted a few small, gray blotches—hamlets nestled on top of diminutive plateaus. Next to them was the sweeping gash of a landslide. Farther down, the silver ribbon of a river snaked across the valley floor, negotiated between clusters of tiny twinkling lights.

The Dalai Lama, holding his prayer beads in his left hand, pointed to one well-lit cluster and said, "The village lights still there." He gestured for me to lean closer to him so I could follow the sweep of the valley as it descended from the Triund saddle to the plains and to the shimmering settlements.

It was five in the morning, a pre-Monsoon Sunday. The Dalai Lama was dressed skimpily for the outdoors at this time of the day. He was not wearing his usual monk's robes. He had on a sleeveless, light orange shirt with a high mandarin collar. The satin-like material shimmered in the early-morning light. An ankle-length, rust-colored sarong was wrapped around his body; around his midriff he had tied his maroon monk's shawl. I had never seen this outfit before. I guessed he wore it from time to time for his morning routines in his residence.

This was the first time the Dalai Lama had invited me up to the roof. A concrete catwalk and viewing platform had only recently been constructed. Below us I could see the pristine grounds, for the most part luxuriant deodar, pine, and rhododendron, of his residential compound sited on the upper lip of a spur.

We didn't stay long on the roof. After about five minutes, we walked back down to the spacious second-floor sitting room and into the Dalai Lama's meditation room. He took off his shoes, padded over to the meditation alcove, and sat down in the lotus position behind his desk.

Almost immediately, Paljor-la, the Dalai Lama's monk attendant, came in with a breakfast tray. He set it down on a low cushion on the floor next to the Dalai Lama. There were a couple of Thermoses, a large glass bowl of porridge, a plate of thick-cut toast, and butter and jam.

The Dalai Lama draped a cloth napkin over his lap and picked up the good-size bowl of porridge. Holding it with his left hand, he scooped up one big spoonful with his right. He held it close to his lips for a few moments, staring into the distance. Then he began. As he ate, he read from a five-inch stack of loose-leaf folios—Tibetan religious text—arranged neatly on the desk in front of him.

Then the Dalai Lama picked up a piece of toasted Tibetan bread, baked fresh that morning in his kitchen, and spread Hero strawberry jam evenly over it. He daubed gobs of butter over the jam before biting into the crunchy bread. For breakfast, the Dalai Lama polished off a large bowl of porridge, two sizable pieces of toast, and at least two mugs of milk tea. While he ate, he focused on his reading and made no attempt to talk to me.

The Dalai Lama likes to eat alone. He invariably gets many breakfast or lunch invitations when he travels overseas. Tenzin Geyche Tethong, his private secretary, does his best to turn most of them down. If the Tibetan leader must have company at mealtimes, he actively discourages conversation while he eats.

At 5:30, the Dalai Lama got up and signaled for me to follow him. We went into his bathroom. An entire wall was taken up by windows. He opened the drapes to expose the mystic grandeur of the ridges. A stack of *Far Eastern Economic*

Reviews sat on a low table next to the toilet. The Dalai Lama turned on the tap and started to brush his teeth.

In my travels with him, I've noticed that he almost always brushes his teeth after a meal. On one occasion, the president and the faculty of Tromso University in Norway had given a formal lunch in his honor. After the meal, the Dalai Lama fished a scarlet-red toothbrush and a small tube of Colgate from his monk's bag and held them high for his hosts to admire, like a fisherman brandishing some prized catch. Still holding the oral implements aloft, he made his way to the washroom, much to the delight of the sixty-odd guests.

Back in the meditation room, the Dalai Lama wrapped his shawl around his middle and sat down on the cushion. It was time for his morning meditation session. But before he started, he decided to give me a sense of the day's agenda.

"After my meditation," he said, "around eight, I think I'll start retreat: some special prayers and meditations. That may last one and a half hour; you can stay. Then I may read. Sit there or here," he gestured to the sitting room, which I could see through the open doorway. "And then lunchtime, around eleven-thirty, here. Afternoon free. Free means some reading. Today Sunday, I have no particular job. Usually change watch straps . . ." The Dalai Lama started to giggle as he fiddled with his watch. "But today I don't think any work. Evening, around five, I take bath. After bath I sit here with towel—like New Guinea people, naked." The ludicrous image triggered a spasm of belly laughs. "At five-thirty, five-forty, my evening tea. Then say bye-bye."

For the first time since I'd known him, he had invited me to spend a good part of one day with him in his private quarters.

The Dalai Lama unfolded the shawl and rewrapped it snugly around his abdomen. He put his prayer beads on his lap, tucked his robes under his folded legs, and pushed his watch up his arm a notch. He straightened his back, rocked forward once, and sat upright. He was ready to begin his meditation.

It occurred to me that the Dalai Lama was not very different from some of the hermits I'd seen in Tibet. The hermits secluded themselves in small caves high in the Himalayas, their daily food delivered to them by faithful attendants. Their only responsibility: to get on with their spiritual practice. When the Dalai Lama sat on his one-square-meter meditation cushion on the floor, he was in his personal hermitage—albeit a well-appointed one. His personal space, hemmed in by a simple desk and a knee-high wooden cabinet topped with a red in/out tray, is reduced to a cubbyhole not much bigger than a telephone booth.

The Dalai Lama reached a deep place in his meditation very quickly, not taking more than a minute or two from the start. His eyes were closed. In his lap, the fingers of both hands were clicking his prayer beads rhythmically. As his meditation progressed, his head drooped. Every so often, I could see his baggy eyelids being buffeted by pronounced rapid eye movement—it was as if a large marble was jiggling back and forth under a handkerchief.

An hour passed. The Dalai Lama, without breaking his meditation, reached into a shelf in the cabinet on his right and switched on a Sony shortwave radio. The BBC World Service came on after the four familiar beeps. It was 6:30 A.M. in Dharamsala, 1:00 P.M. in Greenwich. The lead news story was about the historic meeting between Ariel Sharon, the Israeli prime minister, and his Palestinian counterpart, Mahmoud Abbas. "They met in Jerusalem to discuss the American-backed peace plan known as the Roadmap," the female announcer intoned, her voice resonating loudly in the peaceful meditation room. "The meeting was held in Sharon's heavily guarded offices, and security was the main topic."

The Dalai Lama showed no sign that he was listening. But his body seemed strangely tense. He folded his hands together and pressed the thumb edge tight against his nose. There was exertion in the gesture. It was as if by forcing his palms firmly into his face he'd be able, by sheer force of will, to gain a new level of insight.

Still in meditation, he reached for his sunglasses—the sun had risen above the Dhauladhar ridges, and crisp morning light was pouring into the room. He mumbled a few quick snatches of prayer and then turned off the radio.

Getting up from his meditation cushion, the Dalai Lama walked into the sitting room, a gorgeous space with floor-to-ceiling windows on three sides. The room took up a good half of the second floor. Large clumps of purple bougainvil-lea draped the exterior of the building, softening the late-morning light that streamed into the room. The Dalai Lama went to the far corner and sat down on a cushion on the floor, behind a low table stacked with folios of Buddhist scriptures.

Nearby was a late-model treadmill, a present from a German devotee. It stood in front of a brilliantly lacquered Buddha sculpted from a gnarled piece of tree trunk. I recognized the distinctive image immediately. It was a gift from President Chen Shui-bian of Taiwan; I had been there when he presented it to the Tibetan leader. I imagined the Dalai Lama, if and when he decided to make use of the treadmill, focusing his gaze on the Buddha, much as others might watch their favorite TV show while they exercise.

As the Dalai Lama read from the folios, he made occasional notes on the pages. After about twenty minutes, he got up and moved to an armchair in the opposite corner of the room. I followed and sat discreetly on a straight-backed chair near him.

"Sometimes strange things happen," the Dalai Lama said to me out of the blue. "Fifty-eight. Summer. Precious relics materialized on Buddha's throne in Lhasa's cathedral. I received report and some relics were sent to me in my summer palace. Me: a little doubt, don't know whether genuine or not. The monk who looked after the statue at that time old, fat. Looks dubious character. We always joked about him. So I was skeptical. I sent one official. He put white scarf on place where relics appeared and he sealed. After few days I visited. Opened seal. Oh, lots of relics there, inside a crack on the

Buddha's seat. I think that is a sign, some kind of farewell gift. So fifty-nine, March, we left. Strange, isn't it?"

"What did the relics look like?" I asked.

"White. Looks like small, round pills. Lots. Almost mugful."

He looked thoughtful. He stared out of the window, clicking his prayer beads rhythmically. Then he turned to me.

"You've visited me here many times in the last few years," the Dalai Lama said. "You've traveled with me to so many places. Every chance you get, you asked me questions. Sometimes quite stupid ones . . ." He broke into one of his laughing jags.

He continued: "I like to ask you some questions now."

Ummm . . . OK. This was unprecedented; it was not in the script. I didn't know if I'd be ready for this.

"Of course, Your Holiness. I'll try my best to answer."

"Firstly, since you come to know about Tibet, you visited Tibet," the Dalai Lama began. I could sense his heightened focus on me. As if he was willing some of his one-pointed meditation energy toward me. "You actually carry out some work there. Wrote big book about Tibet's pilgrimage places. What you think of Tibetans?"

"Well, as you know," I replied, "I first came into contact with Tibetans and Tibetan culture when I came to Dharamsala more than thirty years ago. For a Chinese from Hong Kong, used to a fast-paced environment, it was a culture shock. I was surprised by the friendliness of the people. Tibetans laughed easily. And I got the feeling they cared about the people they come into contact with. Even total strangers.

"When I traveled in Tibet, the Tibetans I met there had the same qualities. One thing stood out: they never prejudged me—even though they knew that I'm Chinese. I didn't have to pretend to be Japanese.

"I know there are a lot of romantic, idealistic projections out there about Tibetans. The reality is not like that. Tibetans, like most people, can be devious, materialistic. But having observed them for a long time, I can honestly say: on the whole, the Tibetans' good qualities more than compensate for the bad."

"I think that is general impression," the Dalai Lama said. "Otherwise, time passes, the foreign tourists' friendly attitude may change. But now, after forty-four years, in spite of knowing some drawbacks, some faults, general friendly attitude to Tibetans increasing."

I nodded. From what I have seen, this was certainly true in Dharamsala. More and more tourists were coming. So much so that the Indian government had decided to make a special effort to upgrade the hill station's dismal infrastructure.

"Come sit closer," the Dalai Lama instructed me. I pulled my chair toward him. "Now, eventually we developed some friendship. Not only that. Through the coming book, you're trying to tell people about Tibet, about Dalai Lama. Not propaganda, I don't think. How you feel about book, about our work together?"

I thought it interesting that the Dalai Lama used the word "propaganda." It's something he's acutely sensitive about. All his life he's seen the corrosive effect of Chinese propaganda; it's something he wants to avoid at all costs.

"I don't think the book is propaganda," I replied. "I try to write about things I see with my own eyes. I try to record things as truthfully as possible. But I have to point out one thing. I'm not exactly an impartial, hard-driving investigative journalist. Over the years, I have developed strong ties with many Tibetans. I've a soft spot for you and Tibet. But I try to be objective; I try not to be too starry-eyed."

The Dalai Lama nodded. He took off his glasses and rubbed both eyes with the balls of his palms. Perhaps he was getting tired from listening to my ramblings. I noticed for the first time a wooden cabinet across the room from him. It had a jumble of books and journals. Sitting innocuously among them was a large black shortwave radio—a professional piece of equipment that belonged to an earlier era. A small photo of the Dalai Lama's deceased mother sat unobtrusively on one corner. She was much beloved by him.

Then the Dalai Lama continued with his train of thought. "So all this happened since you developed some contact with me. So now, what change, you yourself?"

This was a subject that I had not thought much about, and I was at a loss for words.

"Well . . . for one thing," I finally said, "I guess you have been my role model. Your ability to forgive. Your kindness to people, even to those you just met; your high moral standards; your altruism. These are the things I see with my own eyes. They set powerful examples for me. But I guess the most meaningful thing for me is this: after some of these ideas have finally sunk in, I was able to share them with my two young children. Hopefully, I make a half-decent role model for them."

The Dalai Lama was perching awkwardly on the edge of the armchair. It seemed to me that, having just spent upward of four hours sitting on the floor that morning, he had difficulty coming to terms with modern furniture designed for ordinary people. He shifted position, trying to lean all the way back against the cushions. It was too much of a stretch. He propped the small of his back against the padded side arm of the chair instead. He looked even more uncomfortable than before.

"I won't say I've become a better person since I started working with you," I continued. "As you have said, these things take time. But I think I've become more aware, more sensitive. I've a sense of the rewards of altruism, for example. If I'm nice to others, I myself will benefit. I've experienced the satisfaction that comes of being considerate to others. I've no doubt forgiveness is in your bones. And I saw that it gives you peace of mind. I also learned something about interdependence. As you have said, 'One thing happens someplace, repercussions hit your place.' So, these are some of the things I've been exposed to. Some may actually have rubbed off, if only temporarily. Now, if I get to do another book with you, there may be real hope for me yet."

The Dalai Lama had a good chuckle over this.

I decided to ask him a question of my own, a question that

had been on my mind for some time. "You have been a Buddhist monk for all your life. Let's not talk about difficult things like nirvana or enlightenment. But what do you want to achieve?"

There was no hesitation. His answer was immediate; it was as if he had been waiting for this. Here is what the Dalai Lama said: "To be happy. My practice helps me lead a useful life. If I can give some short moment of happiness to others, then I feel that my life has achieved some purpose. This gives me deep mental satisfaction—this feeling always comes if you serve others. So, when I help others, I feel happy. For me, the most important thing is human compassion, a sense of caring for one another."

Our interlude over, he stood up and headed back to his meditation room. He sat down behind his desk and resumed his prayers. I sat on a lone, dark red folding chair near the entrance, a few meters from him. The Dalai Lama was in profile. Beyond him, through a wall of glass, were the multiple knife-edge ridges of the Dhauladhar range, now in brilliant sunlight. To my left was the most sumptuous and sacred collection of Tibetan objets d'art ever assembled in one place, all meticulously arrayed within a large glass-enclosed altar. The stunning images—hundreds of big and small statues, centuries-old Tibetan hangings painted in vibrant rock colors, all with legendary provenance—assault the senses. I was conscious of the Dalai Lama's vital energy, his essential goodness permeating all the objects and space in the room, the result of the thousands of hours he had spent in meditation and prayers here.

19.

Sophisticated Mind, Calm Mind

The two Tibetan doctors arrived at the residence for the Dalai Lama's weekly checkup. Dr. Namgyal was the first to appear at the entrance to the meditation room. He prostrated three times to the Dalai Lama from the threshold. Dr. Tseten followed suit. If they were surprised to see me, they kept it to themselves. Their attention was focused squarely on the Tibetan leader.

Dr. Tseten gestured for his colleague to begin. Dr. Namgyal, a slender man in his thirties, was dressed in a long, black robe with a turned-up mandarin collar. A specialist in Tibetan medicine, he knelt on the thick carpet before the Dalai Lama. The Tibetan leader hunched forward, resting his left elbow on his thigh, his forearm upright. The physician placed both his hands gently around the Dalai Lama's left wrist. The fingers on Dr. Namgyal's hand fluttered and danced, as if he was playing the flute; he was probing for subtle, infinitesimal changes in his patient's vital currents. The heads of the two men were nearly touching. One man was clad in the richest shades of maroon and ocher, the other the darkest of black. The two seemed like two large birds of prey, of different species and vastly different plumage, huddled closely together so one could tune in to the heartbeat of the other.

The Dalai Lama said something to the doctor in Tibetan, his voice deep, booming, and uninhibited. Dr. Namgyal responded in the softest of whispers. After a minute or two, he let go of the Dalai Lama's wrist. The Dalai Lama proffered his other hand. This time, the physician used the fingers of his left hand to question the pulse.

When Dr. Namgyal was finished, Western-trained Dr. Tseten approached the Dalai Lama and placed a fluffed-up pillow on his lap. The Tibetan leader rested his right arm across it as Dr. Tseten put on his stethoscope and took his patient's blood pressure. The Dalai Lama chatted with him the whole time: reporting, questioning. It was obvious that he takes an active, informed role in the monitoring and maintenance of his health.

After ten minutes, the doctors left as silently as they had come.

The Dalai Lama moved back to his meditation cushion. He turned to me and said, "Now, more questions."

So he wanted to continue with his interview. I had the

feeling that he was enjoying his new job. He got to ask the questions for a change. For my part I relished the role reversal. It was a new experience. It gave me a chance to interact with my coauthor differently. And it forced me to think about things I had not paid much attention to before.

"You born Chinese family as a Chinese, but grown up in, I think, more Westernized society," the Dalai Lama said.

"Yes, I suppose so," I answered. "For the first twenty years of my life, I lived in a Hong Kong when it was still very Chinese. My mother didn't speak English. Her mind-set, habits were definitely very Chinese. But Hong Kong was a British colony then, and I went to a British school. So I guess I was half and half: Chinese upbringing but also influenced by Western ways."

"Umm . . . umm." The Dalai Lama mulled that over. "Now, you have more contact with Tibetans . . . Tibetans belong to Asia. Buddhism is something common to Chinese as well as Tibetan. So you get more Asian culture."

I was a bit lost. I wasn't sure what he was leading up to.

I made a stab. "I left Hong Kong when I was twenty years old. Since then I'd spent most of my time in the West. But I also have lived in Nepal for four years and visited Tibet many times. Those years in the Himalayas made a strong impact on me. Through my association with Tibet and with Tibetan Buddhism, I'm certainly more appreciative of Asian culture."

"One occasion," the Dalai Lama continued, "Mind and Life Conference. One Japanese, she was observer. At the end of conference, she told me: till now, I always get the feeling, we Asian, of course we have rich tradition, but we have no capacity to do research.

"We always feel that we are just objects of investigation by Westerners. Their scientific-minded people always observe us. We have no capacity to do the same thing.

"After the Mind and Life Conference, then she got the feeling: We Asian, with our Asian tradition, also have the capacity to investigate reality more equal way.

"So do you ever have this kind of feeling? Our own traditions rich, but something ancient. In modern times not much useful, not much catch the time. But West is something very, very high?"

Most of us who grew up in third world countries invariably have this discussion at some point in our life. The West is so advanced; their citizens so rich and smart. We from the East suffer by comparison.

"Well, I grew up in Hong Kong in the fifties and sixties," I replied. "China was known then as the Sick Man of Asia and Hong Kong a cultural desert. Living under the British I had developed a sense of inferiority about Chinese culture—at least about Chinese culture as we knew it in Hong Kong. We were backward technologically, and the gap was widening fast. This was reinforced when I was a student doing physics research at the Enrico Fermi Institute in Chicago. I learned something about quantum theory and atom smashers, and I was in awe."

"So because your new knowledge of Tibet," the Dalai

Lama continued with his line of questions, leaning his upper body forward from his lotus position, "you get more understanding about Tibetan culture and Tibetan Buddhism. These things imply Asian intellectual tradition. So now, do you get stronger feeling: I'm Asian? Something nationalistic feeling? We Asian, we Chinese, we Tibetan. Some kind of more self-confidence?"

The Dalai Lama had never proselytized about Buddhism. He has maintained for decades that we're all better off sticking to traditions indigenous to our own cultural milieu. But now, for the first time since I'd known him, the Dalai Lama seemed to be fishing for compliments. He was like a proud father showing off his firstborn. In a rare moment of candor, he allowed his deep-seated admiration of Buddhism to shine through. I could understand this. After all, he had been practicing for six decades now. He's like an Olympic athlete who, with incredible discipline and brutal training, can finally take his rightful place on the podium. And as I admire the Olympian winning a medal, I do not begrudge him for showing a tiny bit of pride.

"When I met you in 1972," I told him, "I started to develop some curiosity about Buddhism. I dabbled in Zen, Taoism, and Vipassana. In the last few years, thanks to you, I've come to know something about Tibetan Buddhism. Here is what I thought: this two-thousand-five-hundred-year-old system of thought is incredibly pertinent to mankind in this day and age—a genuine treasure. It offers a workable blueprint to emotional well-being. And as scientists have now concluded, it's good for our health too. So, yes, I'm proud that I know something about Buddhism—a wisdom tradition that came out of Asia. As Jean-Jacques Annaud, the movie director, once said: 'Buddhism is everywhere.' And Amazon.com tells me there are now twenty thousand books on Buddhism."

A T 11:30, Paljor-La, the monk attendant, came in with a large, laden tray. He set it on the small coffee table in front of the Dalai Lama, who was already sitting in his corner armchair. There were at least ten assorted plates and bowls. Like many Buddhist monks, the Dalai Lama's most important meal of the day is lunch.

The Dalai Lama was hungry. He had been up since 3:30, and his breakfast had been six and a half hours ago. He leaned forward impatiently and quickly took the lids off the dishes. It was a sumptuous meal, and it smelled wonderful: round Tibetan breads, soup, a few plates of great-looking stir-fried vegetables, a plate of raw radish, and a big serving of what looked like Vietnamese spring rolls. The Dalai Lama eagerly surveyed the spread before him. He grabbed a piece of Tibetan bread and took a bite. As he savored it, he looked up and realized I was standing at a respectful distance, watching him with fascination. He redirected his attention to the dishes before him; then, after a moment's hesitation, he picked up the plate of radish.

"My offering. Take one piece," he said, as he thrust the plate toward me. I dutifully took one.

"Now, last six months, mostly vegetarian," he told me between swallows of soup. "Nearly no more meat except sometimes dry yak meat, from Tibet. I tried vegetarian before, in 1965—for twenty months, remain vegetarian." He put the soup bowl down, and picked up a piece of the spring roll. "Now, not very strict. In big hotels, I enjoy meat."

"Taste," the Dalai Lama said, offering me a piece. The chewy wrap complemented the delicate filling perfectly: slivers of dried yak meat, with its signature intense flavor, mixed with glass noodles and crunchy vegetables. The taste was exquisite. The Dalai Lama obviously had a superb cook.

"Good?"

"Delicious."

The Dalai Lama nodded. "Have a break and come back at five. Thank you, bye-bye."

WHEN I RETURNED to the Dalai Lama's residence at five that afternoon, he was again sitting on the meditation cushion behind his desk. A pale yellow bath towel was wrapped around his torso, and his rust-colored sarong was bunched up around his hips and legs. The TV, a late-model Sony Wega, usually concealed in a cabinet to one side of the altar, was now turned on, its volume low. The Dalai Lama, his right hand on the remote, was watching the Discovery Channel intently. A majestic three-mast Chinese junk, sailing in the South China sea, was tacking deftly between emerald islands. After a minute or two of this, he switched channels. BBC World presented the latest satellite weather report.

His eyes still glued to the TV, the Dalai Lama asked me, "Do you know how many people in Hong Kong over one hundred? Recently I met people whose age above ninety in Tawang, around fifteen. One place I met one man. I asked how old and he said a hundred, but looks like around sixty."

"My father's father was over ninety years old," I fudged in reply. I had no idea of Hong Kong's statistics on age distribution. "Even though he was a confirmed opium addict." The Dalai Lama seemed slightly taken aback by this piece of information, not sure whether to believe me or not.

"And Sikkim also, I noticed," he continued. "I met few above ninety and one above a hundred. One nun, a few years back when I was there, told me she was a hundred. She looked seventy, like that."

"Peace of mind," I said, referring to the Dalai Lama's conviction that peace of mind can lead to a long and healthy life.

"I think their lives more simple," the Dalai Lama said. "Peace of mind, no doubt there. Peace of mind two ways. One: life quite simple. Because of that, mind less disturbances. Another: mind very sophisticated; mind knows many things. But inside that, mind calm." He pointed a finger at his nose and said, "Like me." He tilted his head back and laughed long and hard.

"But how do you achieve this calm mind?" I asked the Dalai Lama.

SOPHISTICATED MIND, CALM MIND

"Analyze," he said simply.

"Analyze?"

"For example, look my very bad stomach pain in Patna. I analyze situation. If some possibility to eliminate the pain, then no need to worry—because there is solution. Now, if no solution, then also no need to worry—because you can't do anything. Another thing. It is very useful to compare the pain to some even bigger pain. You right away get the feeling, 'Oh, this pain is actually not too bad compared to that one.' So you immediately feel better."

The Dalai Lama reached over to the red in/out tray on top of the wood cabinet and retrieved some papers.

"I received one letter from Taiwan," he told me. He unfolded two pieces of paper, searching them for the passage he was interested in. He started to read aloud: " 'I was a man of bad temper. People were often upset by me. As a tea dealer, my greed made me lose profit, and I suffer mental anguish from time to time. Now through learning something about Buddhism, I realize the faults of desire. My bad temper was controlled gradually. I won't easily criticize other people.' " The Dalai Lama put the letter down on his lap, looked over to me, and beamed with obvious satisfaction.

"Then I think one other thing he mentioned." He scanned the page, then read aloud again, " 'And I was doing business one day. All of a sudden, I was considering my competitors' needs more than mine. This is new experience.' " The Dalai Lama looked up, hooted loudly, and continued reading. " 'I never had this in my life. Now my family and friends feel more easy with me and my business improved.' " He scratched his head and laughed some more.

Paljor-la came in at 5:30 P.M. with a tray bearing two Thermoses and a napkin-covered plate. He placed a mug on the Dalai Lama's desk and poured steaming tea into it. The Dalai Lama picked up the other Thermos and topped up the mug with hot milk. As Paljor-la turned to leave, the Dalai Lama lifted a corner of the napkin to peek at the plate's contents. He said something to his attendant, who went around a corner and came back with a large plastic box containing an assortment of crackers. The Dalai Lama rummaged through it carefully. He took his time about it. He finally chose a round cracker and handed it to me.

"So now finish. Thank you, bye-bye," he said. From his cushion, he extended both his hands toward me. I bent down, held his hands in mine, and touched my forehead to them.

"Thank you, Your Holiness," I said.

A question nagged at me as I walked out of the Dalai Lama's residence. What had been on the plate? Something sinful and yummy? The Dalai Lama, like all Tibetan monks, wasn't supposed to eat anything substantial after his noonday meal. I couldn't help smiling as I bit into the cracker—a direct offering from the Dalai Lama.

Acknowledgments

First and foremost, I'd like to thank His Holiness the Dalai Lama. This book simply would not exist without his unwavering support and gentle encouragement. Over the years, I've been extraordinarily blessed to be able to spend long hours in the compassionate presence of His Holiness. I'm honored that he entrusted me with the task of bringing his wisdom into print.

I owe a great debt of gratitude to Tenzin Geyche Tethong, Secretary to His Holiness the Dalai Lama. He enthusiastically endorsed the book from its very beginning. With his trademark grace and thoughtfulness, he has helped me through many a difficult situation.

Ngari Rinpoche offered an abundance of glucose biscuits and hard-to-come-by Coca-Cola in the high-altitude valley of Spiti. He has been a low-key, considerate, and steadfast advocate of the book. I treasure his forthright friendship and our idiosyncratic time together in India, Europe, and North America.

Tenzin Namdak Taklha is the mastermind behind many of my extended tours with His Holiness. In his command of the myriad details involved in these complicated productions he is without peer. I'm indebted to him for his fairness and professionalism in fielding my numerous, oftentimes last-minute requests.

In my Dharamsala interviews with His Holiness, Lhakdor has always sat by my side. I'm comforted by his presence, and I relish his clear elucidation of His Holiness' more difficult teachings. His genuine warmth, great sense of humor, and encyclopedic knowledge of the dharma helped to set the tone of the book.

Over the years, Lodi Gyari, Samdhong Rinpoche, and T. C. Tethong have been unstinting in giving their time to the project. I value their thoughtful conversations and astute advice immensely, and I'm grateful for the friendship of these wise men of Tibet.

The Offices of Tibet in North America, Europe, and Asia helped with the logistics of my travels with His Holiness. I wish to thank in particular Dr. Nawang Rabgyal, Tenzin Atisha, Tsegyam, Kesang Takla, Chhime Chhoekyapa, Tashi Wangdi, and Kelsang Gyaltsen. And in Dharamsala, my thanks go to Jetsun Pema, Tsering Taklha, Chuki Tethong, Dr.

and Mrs. Tseten Sadutshang, and Joyce Murdoch for their generous support and hospitality.

Noah Lukeman, my agent, and Amy Hertz, my editor at Riverhead, took a chance on the book and have been its strong advocates since the beginning. I also want to thank Marc Haeringer and Julie Grau at Riverhead for their dedicated involvement during the final phases of the project. The book has benefited enormously from the astute editorial guidance of Barbara Pulling, Laurie Wagner, and Nancy Pollak.

I wish to express my gratitude to Professor Pitman Potter, Director of the Institute of Asian Research, the University of British Columbia. He was an enthusiastic and early supporter of the book, and he has been a pillar of strength and inspiration during His Holiness' visit to Vancouver in 2004.

Jacquie Massey, a true friend of the family, read numerous drafts of the book. Always cheerful and insightful, Jacquie offered critiques that proved to be indispensable, and I've come to rely heavily on her impeccable sensibilities. My sister Bonnie provided moral comfort and the occasional air ticket. Dr. Howard Cutler and Manuel Bauer have been my traveling companions from time to time. I'm most appreciative of their companionship and goodwill.

Susanne Martin, my wife, was indispensable to the book right from the very beginning. She was the first to read a rough draft and the last to put her stamp of approval on it. She was parsimonious in her praise and compassionate when she had to give me bad news. For more than a decade, she has selflessly embraced all my endeavors, grounded or otherwise. Susanne's contribution to the book was generous and unconditional, and her warmth and lovely presence suffused our household. This book is for Susanne and our daughters, Lina and Kira.

—*Victor Chan*